Bird-Nesting:
Extreme Co-Parenting
After Divorce

Toby Hazlewood

Table of Contents

Foreword iii

Chapter One - Introduction..1
    Approach...5
    Context and Definitions 6
    Is it for us? 9

Chapter Two - Bird-Nest Parenting – How It's set up.........................12
    Co-parenting...12
    The Golden Rules of Shared and Co-parenting 15
    Golden Rules in Summary...15
    The Bird-Nesting Approach 19

Chapter Three - What is Nesting? – Back to Basics............................26
    Does it demand that both parents are custodian for 50% of the
    time? 29
    Do the parents have to get on with each other or have had an
    amicable split? 30
    Isn't nesting confusing for the kids?...31
    Isn't it expensive? 31
    Does it have to be funded 50-50? 33
    Presumably nesting doesn't work if you remarry and have other
    kids?..34

Chapter Four - How It Works – The Logistics.................................36
    Funding the arrangement...36
    Cleaning 37
    Decorating..38
    Standards of tidiness 39

Chapter Five - The Benefits of Nesting..44
    For the kids 44
    For you as a divorced couple..48
    Financial Benefits 51
    Benefits as an individual...59

Chapter Six - The Challenges 70
   Financial challenges 71
   Closer proximity to your Ex...77

Chapter Seven - Practical Considerations and Concessions 99
   Is it viable for us? 100
   What place to use for the nest 107
   Frequency/interval of parent swapping 114
   When it might not be feasible...125

Chapter Eight - What Happens Next?..129

Appendix - Our House Rules: 131

About the Author..134

Other books by Toby Hazlewood 136

Foreword

Thank you for taking the time to pick up this book. That you've done so suggests that you're a person who is open-minded and willing to consider doing things that are out of the ordinary in order to live the best life possible. This book will help you to understand how an extremely unusual and non-traditional means of parenting after divorce can be established. It describes a model of structuring a separated family that can benefit divorced parents and their kids alike; bird-nesting, also known as birds-nest co-parenting.

The simplest way I can describe birds-nest co-parenting is as follows; after divorce or separation of the family unit, instead of the kids moving between the homes of their parents, the kids remain in a single home. The parents take turns living with them and raising them in that home, separately but co-operatively.

It's the most child-centric and progressive means that I can think of for raising the children of divorce, based around putting their needs to the fore. It's also how I've raised my two daughters following divorce from my first wife.

I'm going to assume that unless you've decided to read the book out of pure interest, you are considering divorce or separation from your partner or are already in the midst of the process. Maybe you've been parted for some time and are looking to see how you can improve your divorced family life. I'm further assuming that you've got kids within that relationship and that as well as weathering the split as best you can, you are most concerned to ensure that once the dust has settled and you and your ex have gone your separate ways, you can continue to parent your kids as effectively as possible.

You are rightly keen to minimise the impact of your parting upon their happiness and wellbeing, and to ensure that they are not just another product of a broken home, whose family structure has a defining effect on them forever more for all the wrong reasons.

Divorce can be overwhelming for the vast array of things that need to be sorted out in the aftermath. There's the information that needs to be digested, choices that need to be made and arrangements to be put in place. This extends beyond the split and associated legal process. There are the significant matters of administration, the dividing up of mutual assets such as houses or pension funds accumulated within the relationship, through to the somewhat trivial division of the consumer goods picked up along the way. All of this has to be done alongside working through the emotional pain and recovery.

I contend though that none of these things are as important as deciding on how most effectively to raise your kids in the aftermath of your parting. For all the thought you may put into it, the separated family structure that you put in place in the immediate aftermath of your divorce may not be the most effective for the long-term. Things change, people change, the needs of you and your kids change.

My name is Toby Hazlewood and what I have to share with you is the lessons I've learned in parenting apart from my ex-wife following the break-up of our marriage in 2005 and in the years since. With little in the way of acrimony and two kids borne from our partnership, we determined that their future happiness was our number-one priority. We decided to explore alternative ways of raising them. In the years that have followed, we've learned a lot, enjoyed plenty of highs and suffered many lows and challenges. Through it all we've maintained a focus on raising our kids as best we could.

If I had been faced with the prospect of some targeted and focussed advice on how to raise kids post-divorce, in a non-traditional parenting model compared to those that are largely the norm these days, I would have leapt at the chance to take it. I've also realised after more than 10 years of parenting life since divorce is that as kids grow older and life moves on after divorce, the parenting structure can often benefit from changing and flexing too. This book focuses on the parenting of the kids from failed relationships using unusual and innovative means to give them, you and your ex the best life possible after divorce.

It advocates an approach that is non-typical, but which I contend works, and works well in allowing the needs of the kids and the parents to be met. Done well, I contend it is as-effective (if not more-effective) than raising kids in a traditional relationship; two people who exist in a relationship aren't necessarily guaranteed to make good parents, and it doesn't mean the needs of the kids are always given primary consideration just because the parents remain together.

I could go on further but I know and respect that your time and attention are precious and so I'll leave it there so we can dive straight into the content.

I wish you well and hope that through this book you'll take comfort that everything will be okay for you and your kids.

Toby

Chapter One - Introduction

In 2016 I published a book that had been written as part of the process of rebuilding my life following divorce from my first wife and the events during the years that followed.

At the dawning of the year 2000 at barely 24 years old I found myself a new parent with a daughter to support in a fledgling relationship with my then girlfriend (of little more than 3 months when we conceived). She would become my eventual wife. Five years later, with a second daughter between us and having shared an eventful few years of marriage, we reached the conclusion that our relationship had reached its natural end and we were going to part albeit on reasonably good terms.

You can read the details behind the founding and the failing of that relationship in that book at a future point should you wish. The significant factor in our split was that we were not content to settle for a conventional set-up as far as our separated family was concerned. We wanted more for our kids.

For an initial 18-month period after parting we adopted a more conventional separated family structure out of necessity and practicality.

Our daughters lived for the majority of their time with their Mum and would visit and stay with me a weekends. I found this extremely hard to deal with, and having always been a very hands-on Dad who was involved in all aspects of raising his kids from birth, I struggled to be apart for them for so long.

What me and my ex-wife realised is that whilst relationships and families break up every day, it doesn't always have to come down to acrimony, custody agreements and disputes over visitation rights when negotiating for the future upbringing of the children of the relationship. There is a way that kids can be raised with the involvement of both Mum and Dad that gives parents and kids alike the best possible family environment that can be established; namely via shared or co-parenting where each parent fulfils 50% of the parenting role for the kids.

It is just such a structure that we set out to establish as the framework for parenting of our kids, who were 7 and 3 by the time this arrangement was put in place. The arrangement was maintained for many years unchanged, with the kids living for alternate weeks with me and then with their Mum.

It has also evolved over time as life has moved on; the kids needs have changed and both my ex-wife and I have remarried to other people. The set-up we now employ, which was established when the girls were 12 and 16, and which I expect to last until they've both left home for university is known as *birds-nest co-parenting*, also known as *bird-nesting*, or just *nesting*. From here onwards, I use these terms interchangeably.

After many years of co-parenting where they'd live with each of their Mum and I for alternate weeks, moving between homes on a Monday, we moved to nesting, where the kids stay in one home and their Mum and I live in with them for alternate weeks.

This is not a simple arrangement to establish and it requires considerable forethought, flexibility and resourcefulness in order to make it work. It also demands commitment on behalf of both the parents to doing what is best for the kids above all else.

When we established co-parenting for the raising of our daughters, we had acknowledged the end our relationship as husband and wife, but our relationship as parents to the kids remained and would endure regardless for all time. We determined that it was our priority to give our kids the best possible upbringing as a separated family and I'm assuming that this is your primary aim since you have gone so far as to pick up this book. If we can make it work, then I genuinely believe anyone can.

Often, desire to do or achieve something is completely removed from the realities of whether it will be achievable. I'm painfully aware that when a couple with kids has decided to divorce or separate there are numerous matters requiring careful and meticulous consideration. As such the prospect of wading through a personal and in-depth account of how I established shared-parenting is probably a bit overwhelming and superfluously detailed at this stage. Similarly, you are probably not even aware of bird-nesting at anything more than a conceptual level, and as such you need to understand more than just how to set it up. I'm hoping you'll value a book that has been created as this one has. It's an account of the backstory to how we arrived at nesting for the raising of our kids. It also contains an outline of the key things to consider if you are looking to use the arrangement to raise your kids post-divorce, along with the things we've learned are essential in making it work.

Inevitably, a certain amount of the book is given over to describing how co-parenting works too, and this is a topic that I feel particularly well-equipped to speak about, having used it to raise my kids for most of their lives. Shared and Co-parenting (terms I also use interchangeably) are also somewhat unconventional as a means of raising children of divorce, although I'm pleased to note that they are becoming more commonplace. With them being somewhat unusual, I've shared the essentials of co-parenting within this book too, particularly as these relate to bird-nesting.

When you've decided to part, undoubtedly the first course of sensible action is to consider your options and make some informed choices about how to approach the rest of your lives. One of the most significant challenges for divorcing parents is how to establish a framework for continuing to raise their kids. The methods you'll read about in this book aren't silver-bullet solutions that can be applied without significant work or compromise. Equally though, they are based on common-sense and ideas that should appeal to any well-meaning parent who wants to do the best for their children even if their relationship with the other parent has failed.

Many of the principles within the book will benefit you and your kids (and your ex too!) even if you choose not to establish true co-parenting, or bird-nesting. I urge you to read-on even if at this stage you're not convinced these can work for you. There are many useful principles

4

contained within, that can be applied in *all* separated families.

Approach

This book distils lessons and experiences from my past with a little associated narrative and background surrounding my circumstances. It describes the pre-existing conditions that need to be met and the considerations that need to be made for you to determine if shared parenting will work for you, and whether bird-nesting may be an effective means of living after divorce.

The background and context included in the original book was worthy of inclusion in for a variety of reasons.

It allowed the reader the chance to understand me, who I am and what my priorities in life are; I believe these facts in combination with the circumstances I found myself in were a big part of what had brought me to that point in life.

It illustrated the context within which my shared-parenting arrangement with my ex-wife had arisen and the critical success factors that have allowed it to flourish since.

This book has excluded much of the background since I appreciate that you are likely to have already decided that you are interested in implementing a shared-parenting structure in your lives for the benefit of your kids, at least conceptually. Taking this assumption further, I envisage that you are newly divorced or at least on a path to divorce and sorting out the structure of parenting for your child is just one of the many matters of great significance that you need to resolve in the near future. As such, you are probably looking for a clear, structured and concise *manual* that will guide you rather than a *novel* from which you have to derive the practical steps. The first step is in deciding if it is for you and whether you can make it work.

Context and Definitions

I thought it would be useful to outline a few high level principles for the book to aid in clarity of understanding as you work your way through it.

I use 'divorce' as a general term for those who are divorced, separated or estranged from their partner for the long-term. It is counter-productive to the intention of this book to do anything other than use these terms interchangeably. I believe that the advice and guidance within the book is equally applicable in all circumstances whether the divorced family comprises any number of children, whether of the same (or mixed) parentage, whether born to the couple or adopted. The couple may be heterosexual or same-sex. Fundamentally this book is concerned with catering to the needs of the children of a family within which the parents have decided to part as a couple but are interested in a non-conventional model of parenting where they both retain an active role in the lives of their kids.

If you decide to do further research on the topic (and I'd assume that since you've gone as far as picking up this book, you're planning on seeking further opinions), you may also see the terms shared-parenting and co-parenting used synonymously. Remember, bird-nesting is an extrapolation of co-parenting by definition; I like to think of it as *extreme co-parenting.*

Before we dive into the ins and outs of bird-nesting, I want to clarify the details of co-parenting and shared parenting in case you're in any doubt as to what it means. From my perspective, whatever you call it, the structure amounts to much the same thing, or is at least driven from the same core principles.

To demonstrate these principles, I have outlined below a simplistic (perhaps over-simplified) definition of what I mean by shared-parenting, by outlining a model of the structure. This can be considered as the benchmark against which further suggestions and advice within this book are considered. It describes the model that has evolved for me, my ex and kids over time, and represents that which I believe works best.

That isn't to say it's the *only* model that will work, but it can be used as the starting point from which you may be able to build your own arrangement.

- The children of the relationship spend their time 50% living with one parent and 50% with the other.

- The structure is based around a regular pattern of days (or weeks) when the kids reside with each parent alternately.

- Both parents live in reasonably close physical proximity during the weeks they have the kids. It may be that they each retain a property for the weeks they have the kids, or that they both decide to remain based in the same general area full-time. The underlying premise is that whilst living with either parent the child is able to attend the same school (or nursery, college, child-minder and so-on).

- Each parent strives to meet the financial costs of raising the child independently of support from the other. The divorce will presumably incorporate its own financial settlement anyway, based on either the ability of the parents to reach their own settlement as to the ongoing support that one parent will provide the other, or a court-decreed settlement. The intention is that each parent treats the fact that 50% of the time they have at least one extra mouth to feed, set of sports clubs to fund, and clothes and shoes to provide, as an accepted facet of their lives rather than a marginal cost for which they want to seek recompense from their ex.

- Each parent strives not to rely on the other parent to any extent during the weeks they have the kids. There may well be regular contact between the other parent and the kids, perhaps even a mid-week visit (subject to mutual agreement) but the key premise is that when you have the kids, they are yours to look after, provide for, pacify and cater to the whims of. You are parted from the other parent and should have no intention or expectation that they are there to support you when you have the kids any more than you will do the same when the kids are with them. This isn't a means for exerting a grudge, but rather to enforce that the parenting team isn't one of Mum and Dad together, but rather two separate parts of the same machine that work independently to achieve the same end goal.

- The set-up is structured, formal and repeatable in that both parents and the kids stick to a regular pattern, usually one week with one parent, the next week with the other, and so-on. The specific details such as whether the kids move between homes on a Monday, a Friday or whatever are somewhat irrelevant. The point is that it is structured and planned ahead and built into calendars. Aside from flexibility to juggle things around a bit at special times of year (such as Christmas and other religious holidays) and to accommodate school holidays and vacations, our schedule of calendars has been built into our diaries for at least the last 5 years without variation; one week on, one week off, switching on a Monday.

There are many other aspects to a co-parenting set-up, but those summarise what I believe we are striving for at a fundamental level.

Bird-nesting builds upon 'standard' co-parenting. It is further defined by the same basic arrangement but whereby the kids stay in one place, a single home, and the parents are the ones who move in and out, on a structured schedule (e.g. alternate weeks), each living elsewhere when they're not living with the kids at the *nest*.

Is it for us?

Each and every aspect of shared-parenting should be informed by a number of core principles. I'm not overstating the value of these when I describe them as Golden Rules and at this stage and in the context of this book, you will have to take a leap of faith in believing that they have been derived through years of experience. The background to the emergence of each of these rules is contained in my first book if you decide you are sufficiently interested to learn more, or want to challenge whether they are valid or not.

The rules are listed in the next chapter for ease of reference.

I believe that an honest consideration of each of these rules and an assessment of how well you think you may be able to adopt them in your life after divorce will help you to decide whether shared-parenting is for you or not.

Just as the concept of shared-parenting is non-typical, I believe it's also advisable to treat the approach as something that you can pick and choose from to an extent. What I mean is that in practical terms you may not decide on a 50-50 split of parenting. This doesn't mean that you can't adopt shared-parenting principles into your separated family as a means of bettering all your lives. In this instance, the kids may not spend 50% of their time with each parent, but rather 70% with Mum and 30% with Dad, and so-on.

I contend that any model where the kids can spend more than alternate weekends and the odd-night here and there with Dad (or Mum) and where the parents can communicate, be seen to make decisions jointly, punish and reward the kids jointly and be seen to each want to play an active part in the kids' lives in spite of being divorced, is advantageous for the kids over a traditional separated model of parenting.

If co-parenting does seem appealing to you, then a possible next step is to consider whether bird-nesting may work for you all too. The book will describe how it works, what's involved in setting it up and maintaining it, and that should help you to figure out if it's for you or not.

Chapter Two -
Bird-Nest Parenting – How It's set up

There are two elements of bird-nest parenting in the context of this book and I think that both are worthy of a description and a bit of discussion about why they are the way they are and how they came about. The two aspects of it are the model of parenting that we employ (co-parenting) and the context within which we apply that model of parenting; within the bird-nest model.

I think it's important to understand the context within which we've chosen to raise our kids, and the core principles that inform co-parenting so that you can further understand the nesting model, why and how it seemed like a natural progression.

Co-parenting

When I wrote the books on co-parenting, with around 6 years' experience at the time to reflect upon what made it work, I identified a series of what I termed 'Golden Rules'. These were the key principles which underpinned the set-up and which I believe were responsible for it being largely successful.

Co-parenting has been the model we've employed to raise our kids from the ages of 7 and 3, to 18 and 14 (at the time of writing) and I feel justified in describing it as a success. Our daughters are happy, loving and academically and socially accomplished young women. They've both achieved great things in their lives and their Mum and I (and their wider family) are extremely proud of them. It's not to say that either of them has been immune to the trials and tribulations that any teenager faces growing up in today's world, but both have weathered the challenges that their peers all seem to have faced, and they've coped as well as them too. Fundamentally they are certainly no worse off than any of their friends who have been raised in conventional non-separated families, by all measures that I can identify as being relevant and meaningful.

A further indication of success has been in the arrangement affording both their Mum and I the space and time to move on and to build new lives for ourselves. Of course we had our differences that were serious enough for us to call time on our relationship. That said, we wish each other no harm and have each gone on to remarry happily to other people, and built successful careers alongside maintaining our commitment to the kids. Of course there have been difficulties and disagreements along the way and doubtless there will be more of these, but taken as a whole the arrangement has worked well for all concerned.

The structure has remained much the same since we first put it in place in Autumn 2007. In brief, the girls have remained in the same school system that they were both in when we split. They've lived a consistent pattern of alternate weeks with each of us, largely uninterrupted except for seasonal variations around summer for occasional 2 week breaks with their Mum or I, and at Christmas when they've generally alternated between us from one year to the next. They've always switched between homes on either a Sunday evening or a Monday evening, since we recognise that structure and consistency are important to us all. The girls have always had a space at each home to call their own, whether it was a shared bedroom or a room of their own, and this has been filled with their own possessions so that they've never felt like guests or visitors but rather that each place was home to them.

We've tried to minimise the impact of the weekly transition by limiting the amount of stuff that would be carried back and forth between the two homes and this has been a particular challenge (which you can read more about in my other books and later in this one). Suffice to say that with the multitude of electronic chargers for the various devices that are ubiquitous these days, along with the wide array of clothes and cosmetics that a teenage girl needs at her disposal, it's been among the biggest challenges to stay on top of.

When they're living with their Mum, she's responsible for meeting their upkeep, feeding and clothing them, taking them to appointments and events that fall in her weeks and I've done the same when they are with me. We've endeavoured to be as self-sufficient as possible and avoid calling on each other for favours and certainly not for baby-sitting (as easy and appealing as that might have been at times). It's been crucial to maintain the boundaries to ensure there's no confusion for the kids about the situation.

We've jointly attended meetings at school, music concerts, sporting competitions and so-on where possible and desirable to the kids. We have jointly and equally funded extraordinary expenses such as school trips, supplies and other occasional costs. My ex gives them allowance, buys them treats and gifts as she sees fit and I do the same. We experimented for a while in giving them joint birthday and Christmas gifts but abandoned that other than for larger items (like bicycles and computers as they got older). We still keep each other appraised of gifts that we buy, but mainly to ensure that they're not spoilt and to avoid duplication.

These may seem like random elements to call out in the description but I use them to illustrate that broadly the core-principle of the approach is to do everything as equitably and co-operatively as possible without blurring the line that we are no longer together. The girls know how it works, and it seems to work well for them and for us.

The Golden Rules of Shared and Co-parenting

As mentioned above, the golden rules have emerged over time and I offer these below as my personal guidelines for a happy and successful separated parenting structure. They're pretty self-explanatory and hopefully in knowing a little about the way our lives are structured as described above, you can see how it all works.

Golden Rules in Summary

Golden Rule #1 – Each and every action, decision and guiding principle must be based around the needs of the kids and what is best for them.

Golden Rule #2 – The fundamental basis of the shared-parenting arrangement must be structured, repeatable and enduring in its design to allow it to benefit the children (see Golden Rule #1) and to meet the needs of the parents.

Golden Rule #3 – In combination with rigidity and structure, a shared-parenting arrangement must be able to flex as the needs of the child and the circumstances surrounding the arrangement (either short or long term) change.

Golden Rule #4 – Once Golden Rule #1 has been satisfied, it is okay for the shared-parenting arrangement to be designed for the mutual and individual benefit of the parents. Ensure though that it is equally beneficial otherwise resentments and negativity will creep in.

Golden Rule #5 – In agreeing the terms of a shared-parenting arrangement, there must be a consideration of the overall sustainability of the arrangement, and the effects it will have on the quality of life of the kids and the parents. If the terms of the arrangement require excessive compromise, expenditure, travel, or efforts to be made on a long-term basis then it is likely that the arrangement will at some point cease to work for everyone and may ultimately fail.

Golden Rule #6 –The financial terms of a shared-parenting arrangement should always be negotiated, reviewed, managed and implemented separately from any other financial arrangements associated with the dissolution of the relationship. Treat any on-going payments that are not split equally between the parents as being focussed on the kids and maintain this distinction. Review the arrangement regularly and strive for an equitable 50/50 split.

Golden Rule #7 –Once you have agreed to move forwards with the shared-parenting arrangement, establish it and immediately start living it (or do so as soon as it is realistically viable to). Apply the same approach to other key decisions, changes and in dealing with events that will doubtlessly occur and need to be managed throughout the arrangement. The time for action is always NOW.

Golden Rule #8 – It is advisable to think about a structured way of doing things, to help adapt to and maintain the shared-parenting arrangement, in as much or as little detail as you feel appropriate to yours and your kids' needs. Expect though that your structures and rules may be different from those of your ex, and don't feel pressured to adapt to their way of working. The key thing is that your overall goals, beliefs, aspirations and priorities for your kids are aligned which will ensure that your kids have a consistent parenting experience across both homes.

Golden Rule #9 – Whilst both parents are unlikely to agree on all matters that require a united-front of parenting, the key thing is to agree on the over-arching principles that shape your shared-parenting arrangement. Within this, matters such as expectations for the kids' behaviour, your aspirations and goals for them, the freedoms and disciplines you want them to grow-up with and the priorities for their upbringing should be understood and agreed upon by you both.

Golden Rule #10 – Where possible, agree on an approach to presenting a united front that ensures a level of trust and autonomy is given by Mum and Dad to each other to deal with the day-to-day in line with the overarching principles of the shared-parenting arrangement. In addition to this, ensure that you both agree with and understand the means by which you will handle the more serious or complex matters and ensure that you devote adequate time to this process.

Golden Rule #11 – Communication between you and your ex is CRITICAL to the successful maintenance of your shared-parenting. Ensure that you are able to discuss matters in a manner and with due consideration, time and sensitivity depending on the issue at hand.

Golden Rule #12 – Both of your children's places of residence should feel like and be treated as their homes. This sense should come about through both places being physically decorated to feel like home, with as few of their possessions following them about as possible to encourage a sense of permanence and belonging at both homes. A few basic principles can be adopted to ensure that the transit of 'things' between homes is kept to a minimum

Golden Rule #13 – It is imperative that you protect and preserve the sanctity and structure of your shared-parenting arrangement as you would protect your kids themselves. Do not allow yourself to be swayed by others be they friends, family, new partners or acquaintances in terms of being forced to modify any aspect unless it is specifically for the benefit of the children. In this case, such changes should be discussed and agreed with the person whom you share the parenting with.

Golden Rule #14 – As you enter into new relationships, and indeed as you contemplate any major life changes, ensure that you are being 100%

true to yourself and ensuring that you don't waver on the things that are essential to you in living the life you want. Failing to do this will impact upon your happiness as a person, and on your ability to be the parent that you want to be to your kids.

I believe that the Golden Rules are pretty self-explanatory and furthermore they have stood the test of time, in raising our girls from little more than toddlers, up to the age where the eldest is shortly leaving home to go to University. It's the principles within these Golden Rules combined with our commitment to give our kids the best possible upbringing and not one that was second best, that's been responsible for this in my view.

The Bird-Nesting Approach

Bird-nesting is a means of building upon the principles of co-parenting, and taking the logistical arrangements for it to the most child-centred extreme possible. We adopted equal co-parenting from two separate homes around 18 months after my ex and I first divorced, and had operated this pattern for over 10 years before bird-nesting was first considered as a possibility. This wasn't for any reason other than a lack of awareness of the possibility.

The concept of bird-nesting was originally suggested to me by my ex around the time my daughters were 11 and 15 years old; I willingly give her the credit for suggesting the idea. I don't know if she became aware of it conceptually or if it was an idea of hers that just happened to already be a recognised structure. It was originally suggested when we were both in well-established new relationships; I was already re-married and she was engaged to do the same. At the time she made the suggestion, I recall that I was hesitant about entering into the arrangement. She had suggested that the rental property that she was maintaining in the town where the girls go to school would be ideally suited to allowing us each to live there during our respective custodial weeks. It was a big house, with enough bedrooms that each of us could have our own space; we wouldn't ever both be living there at the same time, but rather the girls would reside there full-time, and my ex and I would live-in with them for alternate weeks. For the rest of our lives, when not living with the girls as custodial parent of the week, we would each be off living with our new partners in what had become our other new family homes.

The property also had two living rooms that meant we could each have our own living space when there, decorated, equipped and appointed in our own tastes. Later in the book I'll go through the considerations regarding what makes a property suitable for nesting in greater detail since there are a few things that need to be evaluated besides the standards of décor and number of rooms!

As much as I knew that there were financial savings to be made through the arrangement, and prospective benefits for the kids, I was reluctant to move forward with it. On reflection I think this reluctance existed within me for a few of key reasons:

1) I was initially fearful that my new wife would be uncomfortable with the setup.

2) The property proposed to be used as the nest would always feel

like my ex's former home rather than a 'neutral' base that was obtained specifically for the purpose.

3) I worried that the arrangement would potentially be confusing for the girls and hard to adapt to the new way of living.

4) I was concerned that the close-proximity with my ex and the potential for more regular interaction might prompt difficulties, arguments or disagreement, an overall concern that many cite in regard to nesting as a whole.

5) I wasn't sure I wanted to live with such close visibility into the life of my ex; even though I knew I fully intended to respect her privacy and trusted that she'd respect mine, I was still concerned that as a result of sharing a space (even if we were never there at the same time) it would feel a little too close for comfort, and offer reminders of our past.

Some of these concerns were obviously fairly trivial objections in the wider scheme of things, and certainly not in line with many of the golden rules of our co-parenting arrangement, in that we were still striving to give the kids the best upbringing possible and to put them first. I felt though that some of the concerns were worthy of some thoughtful consideration before committing to (or rejecting) the idea.

The proposed setup would certainly have saved us money on rental costs (I was also renting a property locally for use solely when the girls were with me by this point). The financial savings would have undoubtedly improved the quality of life for us all. Additionally, I'm sure the girls would have immediately appreciated the setup in not having to move between homes.

Objection number 1 above was also pretty groundless. On discussion with my new wife it was apparent that she thought the idea made sense too. I guess that my initial reaction was driven by male pride, ego, or just innate inflexibility! It's entirely feasible though that a new partner would feel uncomfortable with the idea, and so I'm relieved that I wasn't considered outlandish by my wife for raising this.

With a few months passing to allow me to live with the idea, I came around to thinking it probably made sense, and could also see the merits of moving into that particular property given the space that it offered. It's ironic then that when I decided to revisit the discussion with my ex on a handover day, it happened to coincide with her landlord having advised her that they were going to sell the house and she'd have to move out!

At that point, we had both committed to the idea of nesting in principle, and agreed that after the summer vacation we'd begin a search for a property to use as the nest. The specification for the nest for our separated family follows. Bear in mind that we had no idea of how the whole process would work but knew that we'd be there alternate weeks with our two daughters:

1) It needed to have a minimum of 3 bedrooms, ideally 4 (one for each of the girls and at least one room for the 'parent of the week', but ideally one each for each of the parents; more on this later)

2) It needed to be within comfortable walking distance of the girls'

schools and bus-routes to the local 16-18 college where our eldest was about to start studying.

That was basically it. I know it sounds overly simplistic, but therein lays the point. Nesting doesn't rely on any specific kind of property being available, or on a specialist location or anything else. When the new school year came around we felt that there was no time like the present (in line with Golden Rule #7 above) and decided that we'd trial the arrangement using my existing rental property.

As it turned out, the arrangement worked out well from the very beginning. The only issue however, was that the property in question actually had a really tiny amount of floor space. I'd been trying to save money to eventually buy a new property and had taken out a rental on the smallest 3-bed home I could find at the time. While this place was undoubtedly a stop-gap that I could put up with, when it came to some of the demands of nesting that have emerged (more on these later in the book), it was simply just too small and not fit for purpose.

A few months later and we moved on with the arrangement. Following a return to the property search, we jointly took out a rental on what I consider to be the ideal kind of property for nesting. It's a 3-bed apartment, with 3 bathrooms and a large open plan living area and storeroom.

The facilities are relatively incidental and will be discussed later in the book as part of the wider considerations of setting up nesting and selecting a property that works for all involved. In case it helps you to picture the arrangement we operate, in your mind as you read this book, the features that I'd identify as being particularly of value are these:

1) The 'Parents' room has an en-suite bathroom and has a built-in wardrobe with storage and a TV. In virtually every way, including the furnishing, it's like stepping into a budget hotel or motel room. We each keep bedding at the apartment, in our respective sides of the wardrobe. When I move in on a Monday evening I retrieve my bedding from the wardrobe and make the bed. At the end of my week, on the following Monday morning I strip the bed and put the bedding away. My ex does the same in her weeks. We both use the same bed, but with our own bedding. This is no different to the fact that you undoubtedly use the same bed as strangers but with clean bedding when you stay in a hotel.

2) The kitchen has enough storage that we each have some allocated cupboards to store food so that we don't have to cater from scratch each time we're there. We each bring food with us for the week and feed the kid from our own stocks.

3) The home is furnished and decorated in a mostly neutral style, mainly with pictures of the kids and our wider families. Crucially it's not decorated to my style or to my exes (we have different tastes!)

The fundamentals of the situation are as follows:

- There is enough space for each of us and our things not to feel like we're having to be temporary or uncomfortable about being in the nest (we do spend half our lives there, after all!)

- There's enough storage for us to put our things away when we're not there so as not to make each other feel uncomfortable about having to be surrounded by our exes stuff.

- The home is fundamentally our kids home, and she and I just come and go as the live in parent of the week.

That's a really high-level description of our nesting arrangement as it stands. There's loads more to it, both in terms of how it's set up and how it works and I'll dive into the detail of this as we go through the book. However, I wanted to try and paint a picture for you in brief, as to how our situation evolved, how it's set up now and at a very high level, how it works so that you can picture it as you go through the book.

With this quick description in mind, let's go back a bit now so that I can describe nesting in more detail and cover some of the more common questions that get asked when I first tell people about it.

Chapter Three -
What is Nesting? – Back to Basics

Nesting is an unconventional form of separated parenting after divorce. A typical divorce or separation involving kids may result in the two parents each taking on a new home and the kids moving between the two homes for visitation or custody. Bird-nesting puts the emphasis on the kids staying put and the parents being the ones who come and go. In many ways, this should really be the way things are done; the parents decided to split, not the kids so why shouldn't the parents be the ones who put up with the upheaval?

I've read of a variety of scenarios where nesting has been established. There are those where two divorcing parents have retained the family home and the kids reside there, with the two parents securing alternate accommodation for when they are not the parent-in-residence. Then there are the situations like ours, where we've established a new property specifically for the purpose. In any situation, the fundamental factor is in the kids remaining in the same place for most of their time and calling that home. Mum and Dad will each have separate homes for when they're not custodial parent of the week.

There are a whole variety of other features and facets of the arrangement, but that's pretty much it at a simple level.

The premise for establishing bird-nesting is that the needs of the kids are paramount, and both parents are able to put their differences to one side to enable a minimum of disruption from the arrangement. It sounds unconventional and it is very unusual (I have yet to meet anyone else who has implemented a similar arrangement) but the more you think about it, the more it makes sense on a number of levels:

1) **To reiterate, it puts the needs of the kids to the fore.**
   Regardless of the kids' opinions on their parents divorcing, it was undoubtedly a decision of the parents to split up. Why then should the kids be the ones who end up coming and going in order to retain their bond and relationship with the parents when the parents move on with their lives and establish new homes?

2) **It gives the kids a sense of permanence about their home life.**
   In a conventional separated family, even where the two parents remain co-operative and communicative, there will still be two homes. Usually the kids will be accommodated within those, hopefully on a reasonably permanent basis with a dedicated space in each home to call their own. Even then, if they effectively have two bedrooms in two different homes, they're still likely to favour one over the other, will never have all their possessions around them and are likely to feel transient in one or both places. We operated a *conventional co-parenting setup* (I use the term advisedly since I am still aware that co-parenting is

far from the norm, at least among other divorced parents that I encounter) for over 10 years. We aimed to give the girls stability even though they moved between our homes on a structured weekly basis. In spite of our efforts I know that at times they became dissatisfied with having to move house regularly and at times yearned to be in one place or another.

3) **It enables the parents to move on and build new lives while giving adequate commitment to the needs of the kids in a set context.** I've remained committed to continuing my parenting role to my daughters since the day we split, but my life has moved on. I've changed careers, advanced my business ventures, travelled and ultimately met and married my second wife. Throughout all this, I've been consistent in showing up to my role with my daughters and that remains constant. Having that grounded in a single place, first in my home when we were co-parenting and the girls moved between my home and their Mums, and now in the 'nest' has allowed this to be fulfilled with consistency and routine. In parallel with meeting the needs of my kids, I've been afforded the space and time to move on and build a new life. The girls are of course a massive part of that, but it's been easier to do as a result of first co-parenting and subsequently, nesting.

There are many other benefits and ways that nesting makes sense the more you explore the concept. These will emerge during the remainder of the book.

Before we go into greater depth on how it works, what you need to put in place to establish the structure and the lessons, benefits and potential pitfalls, I wanted to address a few of the common concerns and queries that are often raised. Again, some of these will be explored in greater detail later on, but they warrant a bit of upfront consideration from the off.

What has struck me throughout my life as a parent post-divorce, is that no matter what you do, and no matter how well-meaning your choices and decisions are, there will always be those who are critical of you and the things you do. They will ask questions and present opinions, and even those that are well-meaning can often feel unwelcome. A positive side-effect of this is that for all the questions and challenges, I've now got well-rehearsed responses that aren't just defensive, but are honest and based on my experience.

Here are some of the challenges I've heard.

Does it demand that both parents are custodian for 50% of the time?

No. Our arrangement throughout our co-parenting has always been that we each have custody for a week at a time and we've preserved that for the nesting arrangement too. This has lasted from when the kids were barely at school, through to adulthood where the eldest is now leaving home in a couple of months to go to University. When I move out on a Monday morning, my ex moves in later that day. The nesting arrangement would work equally well though if I fulfilled a more typical *divorced father role* and mainly had the kids for alternate weekends and the occasional mid-week visit, where my ex moved out to alternative accommodation for the nights when I was the custodial parent. 50-50 has been our model, but it's not essential. The crucial element is of course that the kids remain in the same home, and the parents move in and out around them, no matter what the schedule is.

Do the parents have to get on with each other or have had an amicable split?

The obvious pre-requisite is that both parents are keen to have an active role in the raising of the kids, but it's not essential that they both get on well with each other. I consider myself to have had an amicable split and I'm grateful for that. With that said, we still had our differences (and still do from time-to-time) and of course were sufficiently unhappy together to decide to part. This is certainly not an absolute pre-requisite though. Clearly it won't work if you hate each other's guts and are constantly trying to concoct ways to exact revenge on each other. There are many ways in which you inevitably get a closer insight into their lives (such as through the things around the nest that remind you of their proximity). In theory, and generally speaking, in practice there's no reason why you should ever have to encounter them in day-to-day life. I see my ex maybe once every two or three months, mostly when this has been planned (such as when we're both attending an event at one of the kids' schools). That too could be completely avoided if we needed it to be.

Aside from a mutual commitment to the kids, you both need to have a desire to act as fair, reasonable and sensible people and to demonstrate a bit of civility towards each other too, ideally. I'm assuming if you've gone as far as exploring this concept you are at least smart enough to realise that nesting isn't an opportunity to financially rip-off your ex, sabotage their possessions or to exact any other revenge on them. It's a means of putting your kids first.

Isn't nesting confusing for the kids?

I don't see why it would be? Our kids have grown up knowing that their parents were divorced. In fact, I suspect that the youngest has no recollection of a time when we were together; we parted when she was almost 3, and the eldest was 7. We've co-parented them 50-50 for nearly all the time since, and whilst they recognise that we're both civil and polite towards each other, they know that neither of us harbours any ambition to be back with the other. They have plenty of friends whose parents have parted and see the different (and less co-operative) custody arrangements that are in place for them. Indeed, my second wife has two kids from her first marriage, who are step-siblings to my two. Their arrangement with their Dad is quite different and more conventional for a separated family with more sporadic contact between them and him. I often wonder what comparisons they make between their lives and those of my daughters (and vice-versa).

The setup is only confusing for the kids to the extent that it's non-typical. I don't know if my daughters have ever bothered to explain it to any of their friends and I suppose that in the eyes of other kids it could seem unusual. I've never been aware of it being an issue for either of them though.

Isn't it expensive?

Everyone will have their own definition of *expensive* and part of what makes divorce in itself into an unpleasant process at times is the financial angle. I'll explain in more detail how our nesting arrangement evolved as this book progresses. For the purposes of this question, nesting has actually *saved* us money. When we split, we each took on a new home and the financial arrangements between us saw that we were each able to fund the homes independently. We remained in the same town and the kids stayed at their schools, switching between our homes each week. Over time, we each met new people and eventually remarried to other people.

Neither of us harboured long-term ambitions to live in the same town as the kids go to school for the longer term, and each of us has established a new permanent home in a new town around an hour in opposite directions from where our kids were at school. To continue to deliver on our co-parenting commitment until the kids reach adulthood meant that we each retained a second home that was used for the weeks when the girls were with us. These homes each sat empty for a week in-between times. As described earlier, when we first considered nesting, we were going to give up one of the two homes and split the costs, but neither property was suitable (I've suggested a specification for an ideal nest later on). We've since gone on to find and secure a new property specifically for the purposes of becoming the nest, and as such are now saving money compared to our past combined expenditure.

I offer this detailed explanation to illustrate how it works for us. I know that it's been made possible to an extent, by the fact that both me and my ex are lucky enough to have relatively well-paid jobs that offer us both the facility to make this work. However, I'm assuming that if the basic criteria were that a divorcing couple was going to establish two 'family homes' each with space for the kids to visit, then the cost of one 'family home' and two one-bed or studio apartments would likely be of a comparable price in most property markets. At the very least, I doubt the marginal cost is likely to be that much greater. I've included some illustrations later on to help you see what I mean in financial terms.

Does it have to be funded 50-50?

This isn't essential. The complexities of reaching a financial settlement in a divorce where nesting is pursued, versus a traditional one would be no different in my view (although I'm not a lawyer). If the benefits of nesting are appealing to you then the best advice would be to discuss the financing of it to establish if you can make it work. Our situation is made simpler by the fact that neither of us pays money to the other following our divorce, to offset a gap in earnings between us. Neither pays maintenance to the other since we both have the girls for 50% of their lives. We have always each paid 50% towards additional or unusual costs (such as school trips, sporting equipment, school supplies and so-on) and we continue to do so. The nest is funded on a 50-50 basis too, as we each have the use of it for half the time.

At a simplistic level I'd suggest that whatever financial settlement you have in place outside of nesting would presumably remain fair in a nesting context. You'll each have the kids for the same amount of time as has been agreed between you, and would each contribute on the basis of that ratio to the costs of the nest. I'll illustrate a few financial scenarios in a later chapter to demonstrate how this could work in practice.

Presumably nesting doesn't work if you remarry and have other kids?

We're definitely straying into bespoke territory now where each individual scenario will bring additional complications. However, like everything, it can be made to work if you put enough time, energy and forethought into it, and then take appropriate action.

I didn't think I could build a career in project management and management consultancy if I was going to be a single-parent with sole caring responsibility for my two kids half the time. However, I've made it work and have had many project roles where through careful diary management and forward planning I've worked away in distant cities and even overseas for half the time, as has my ex. In the context of developments in life after divorce, I'm now remarried and my second wife has two kids from her first marriage. I live with them in the family home when I'm not live-in parent with the girls, and then I live in the nest the rest of the time. It's unconventional but then so is this entire arrangement. Again, I'll discuss some other theoretical arrangements and how I think they could be made to work with nesting, later in the book. The point here and now, is that in many scenarios and set-ups that will occur in your life after divorce, co-parenting and nesting can be made to work if you're willing to put in the thought and planning to make it so.

These are a few of the more common objections and questions that I've encountered to nesting over time. I will address others later in the book.

It strikes me that like anything unusual, nesting seems to encounter more than its fair share of critics and commentators, often from those who are neither divorced parents or even closely associated with divorced parents. As such I can only put the strength of opinion down to the fact that it is an unusual and progressive way of handling things. Just because it's not typical, it doesn't make it wrong or weird. In any case, it's really down to those who employ it in their lives (you and me!) to feel good about it and to know that it works for them. What anyone else may think or feel about it is really rather irrelevant.

In the next chapter, I'll describe how our nesting arrangement has been set up in more detail so that I can then explain how it works.

Chapter Four -
How It Works – The Logistics

I've already described the property that we use for the purposes of
nesting, and I've outlined the space requirements and the approach we
have to nesting at a high level. In this chapter I want to dive into more
detail regarding the specifics of how it works day-to-day as well as my
thoughts and experiences on some things that are perhaps harder for
others to understand.

Some may appear to be in a mundane level of detail but if you get as far
as implementing nesting in your post-divorce family life then you'll
probably understand better why I've called these out specifically!

Funding the arrangement

We both contribute equally to the costs of the property, the rent, utilities,
Internet and TV service and to cleaning products, and we both use them
to maintain the property. Neither of us checks if the other person has
used their washing detergent, coffee or teabags (as far as I'm aware!) and
we operate on an honour system if we have to borrow something
unexpectedly. I know that on occasion if I've used something of hers as a
last resort, then I'll replace it and I trust that she does the same. We don't
have a contract that binds us to this, but instead we behave as adults

about it.

To do his requires a certain amount of implicit trust between you and your ex as to whether you're to be able to live with the arrangement and relax about the day-to-day financial risk. Only you will know if you trust your ex in paying their way and in not leaving you financially exposed. For the purposes of paying bills, rent and so-on we've chosen to spare anyone else (such as our cable company and utilities suppliers) the pain of trying to understand the ins and outs of the situation. We shared out the registration of accounts with utilities companies, landlord, TV and phone company and so-on between us equally, just the same as others do in a house-share. We also provide visibility of bills to each other and square these up between us on a monthly basis or whenever payment is due. We trust each other to pay their way.

As I mentioned in the financial terms of our divorce we are completely 50-50 about the finances and this means we've become used to splitting costs that come up, equally between us. That this is 50-50 shouldn't mean the same principles can't be applied in your life if (for the sake of argument) one of you pays 70% of child related expenses and the other 30% due to a difference of incomes. The point is that you each pay your way consistently with the other terms of your parenting, and life after divorce.

Cleaning

We both clean the property at the end of our week so that the apartment is presentable and tidy for the other to move into on the following week.

We both enlist the girls to assist in this (with varying degrees of success and co-operation). They're responsible for cleaning their own rooms and bathrooms on a regular basis too. There can occasionally be some overlap between us, for example she may put some washing out to dry before she moves out on a Monday, and I may end up getting the kids to put it away on her behalf. She may leave the dishwasher running with the last of her dishes on a Monday morning and I empty it. I may forget some food in the fridge that goes rotten and she has to throw it in the garbage bin. These somewhat trivial examples are presented as illustrations that you cannot completely isolate each other from having been in the nest before them.

The purpose of cleaning is not to forensically remove all traces of ourselves or each other from the home when we're there. It's about being respectful, cleaning up after ourselves and trying to keep the nest in a good state of order. The ultimate beneficiaries of this are, after all, our kids who get to live in a clean and tidy environment, as well as ourselves. A side-effect of this approach is that they hopefully observe two adults who are demonstrating the traits of being respectful to others, and responsible in tidying up after themselves. I'm as yet unconvinced that this example has completely gelled for my kids given the states of chaos that they seem to live in, but that is beside the point!

Decorating

For the flexibility we have, I don't believe either of us has sought to put our mark on the property in terms of décor and furnishing. It is decorated neutrally and is modern and tidy. I have no burning desire to make it more aligned to my taste and I'm fairly sure she feels the same. Nobody likes to feel temporary about where they live but we both know that this is the kids' home first and foremost. If it's adequate for their needs for now, then that's what's important. Functionality is key and we both have alternate weeks in our own homes to be in our own environments decorated to our own tastes.

With the fundamental purpose being that it's the kids' home, what has made sense is for it to have pictures of them and all the various sides of their family around them. I never took issue with them having pictures of their Mum around them in their bedrooms when we were doing the pure co-parenting and the same was true in reverse. That trend has continued into the nest and to that end the kids have pictures of their wider family from both sides on the walls of the apartment.

Aside from this, we've equipped and furnished the apartment to make it as comfortable for us all as any parent would want their home to be for themselves and their kids. I've purchased a coffee machine for the nest and she's welcome to use it. She's put a TV into the parents' bedroom and I use that on occasion. The point is that we have mutually sought to make the place a comfortable and functional home and we value it as such.

Standards of tidiness

One topic that I'd like to explore in more depth is how the nesting arrangement carries with it a requirement for the kids to adapt to the way of life of the parent in residence depending on which is there for the week. This is something that has been a particular learning point for us all as we've lived with the co-parenting arrangement, and later with nesting.

The kids used-to have to adapt when moving between our homes for alternate weeks, and I suspect that the physical move from one home to the other made it easier in some ways for them to make the mental shift between Mum's Rules and Dad's Rules along the way. It's an inevitable difference between their Mum and me that we have different ways of life and demand differing degrees of order in our homes. That is just the way it is. These standards reflect our own standards and behaviours and I know that mine are different to hers, just as mine are different to those of my second wife too. I'm not saying their ways are wrong or that mine are either.

Speaking for myself (and depending on your own preferences you'll either think me perfectly normal or an utter freak), I like to maintain the home in a standard of general order, cleanliness and tidiness. I'll clear and wash the dishes after each meal, I put my dirty laundry in the basket ready for washing and I put things away when I've finished using them. One of my pet hates is in wasting time searching for things because they've not been put back where they live, and I suppose that having got used to living in two different homes on a regular basis for at least the last 5 years, I've just found it easier not to lose track of things by maintaining a semblance of order about my life no matter where I live. I sound like the life and soul of any party, don't I! Put simply, I prefer order to chaos, and tidiness to mess at all times.

My ex has a more relaxed way of living than this, and whilst not for dissection in this book, it's fair to say that there are differences in how we like to maintain things. I see elements of her preferences reflected in the way the kids approach life, particularly as they've entered their teenage years and I know that they prefer her way of living over mine! Most notably this comes through in them being more relaxed about their morning routine when they're with her than when they're with me. You can read more about this in my original book on Shared Parenting if you're curious about the differences that emerged in their ways of living at each home!

I've tried to persuade the kids of the merits of my way of living for its own benefit and all I can say is that I feel I'm fighting a losing battle much of the time! Nonetheless, as the nest is my home for half the time too, and while I can't force them to live in better order (less chaos) than they seem to choose to in their own bedrooms, I do set and maintain standards for how the communal space is kept, when I'm there at least.

I'm certain that their Mum is happy for the home to be run consistent with her preferences on the weeks she's in charge and that is really the essence of how we manage things from the perspective of tidiness and order. The kids' bedrooms are their own personal space, and it's for them to manage the state of those as they see fit. As long as dishes are returned before we run out of clean glasses and mugs to use, and as long as they don't expect me to venture into their rooms in search of clothes for washing, it's up to them how they want to live in their own space. Expectations still remain for how they treat the rest of the nest and the communal space, and when I'm in charge for the week it's my rules that apply. Their Mum calls the shots when she's there.

I'm certain that this shifting of expectations and standards on a weekly basis has been a source of challenge for the kids, but I am proud to say that for the most part it has continued to work well.

As a side note, at the infancy of the nesting arrangement, I drafted a list of 'house rules' which I posted in the kitchen, and on the backs of their bedroom doors. It was my tongue-in-cheek, vaguely passive-aggressive attempt at conveying my hopes for how the nest might be treated. At various times, I've been ridiculed for it, or challenged to *'add that to the list of rules'* when trying to get the girls to attend to an unpopular task. I'm not suggesting that this is an essential part of making a nesting arrangement work, and even if you do want to adopt a similar set of house rules, you'll probably want to make it align to your own preferences. That said, I hope the rules as I originally drafted them give you some insight into how our nest is set-up. I've included these in an appendix at the end of this book. Feel free to use, adapt or disregard these as you see fit!

This section has shared just a few of the key logistical concerns of running nesting. As you'll appreciate, the key factors for determining success are that the parents adopt a spirit of respect towards each other, and an adult outlook of personal responsibility in how they conduct themselves as they live in the nesting arrangement. Everyone also has to have a fair bit of flexibility in order to make it work.

Having explored the ways in which it works, you're hopefully forming some idea of whether it could possibly work for you and your separated family. In case you're in need of further reassurance as to why you might want to employ nesting I want to revisit some of the many benefits that it can deliver for you in a little more detail in the next chapter. Even if you're not willing or able to consider nesting at this time, many of the benefits can also be attained through co-parenting, so I hope you'll keep this in mind as an option too.

Chapter Five -
The Benefits of Nesting

Many of the benefits of nesting only emerge once you are living with the arrangement, and I've only been able to identify them through experience of actually living within the arrangement and seeing them emerge. Others are more obvious and I've sought to summarise all of these below.

The benefits largely seem to arise in three areas, for the kids, for the individuals, and as a divorced couple.

For the kids

Less Upheaval
The immediate benefit for the kids is in the inevitable reduction in upheaval and hassle in their lives when nesting is in place. There will of course be emotional pain for them as a result of the divorce of their parents, and any loving parent will want to minimise this for their kids. The pain arises not just from the loss of the conventional structure in their lives, but also from the inevitable comparisons that they are likely to make between their lives and the lives of their friends.

I've learned in my own life that while comparisons with others in virtually any aspect and at any time of life are completely futile and certainly unhelpful, but it doesn't make it any easier to avoid making them. For kids of any age, they will see the differences between their lives and those of their friends when divorce brings about change. They'll observe that their friends' parents jointly attend parent-teacher meetings at school, concerts and sporting events where theirs don't (although we have always done so as much as we could). They may observe that their friends' families attend more family oriented events at weekends than they do. They will also note that their friends generally only have one home and one bedroom.

Nesting isn't the silver-bullet solution to all these woes, but it certainly negates the need for the children to have to be constantly moving between homes. It's not the biggest chore for them to have to do so and ours did for many years of our conventional co-parenting. However, nesting helps kids to have stability in many aspects of life, including where they lay their head to sleep at night.

It's not just the stability of where they sleep, but also that having a single bedroom and home allows them to be surrounded by all their possessions. They are able to have the clothes, toys and gadgets they want, constantly at their disposal rather than having to leave them at Mum's or Dad's house. Then there's the limit of the chance of things getting lost between homes or misplaced in the course of transit. I used to get frustrated at my kids in a misguided direction of anger when they lost things in transit, before I realised that I was the joint cause of them having to move back and forth to their Mum's home in the first place. This is no longer a requirement and consequently there's less hassle and upheaval for them and less chance of things getting lost. I also get blamed less when things go missing!

Good examples set by their parents

The other high-level benefit for the kids is not one that they are likely to recognise directly or explicitly, but it's certainly one that I believe that will benefit my kids and those of anyone who puts the kids' needs at the fore after divorce. It sounds self-congratulatory but I genuinely believe that me and my ex are doing the best job we can of setting them a positive example of behaviour towards them and towards each other in response to our divorce. A father needs to be a good role-model for his kids as to what a man's role is as a father, husband and so-on. A mother has corresponding responsibilities as the role-model of what a woman, wife and mother should be. Nesting aids the demonstration of such positive lessons for the kids. Here's how:

- It demonstrates that parents need to put the needs of their kids ahead of their own.
- It demonstrates that the parents are equally responsible for taking control of their own happiness and for taking sometimes difficult decisions (such as to divorce from an unhappy marriage) if they need to in order to get the best out of life.
- It shows the importance of showing-up to the commitments in your life, of doing what you say you will do and fulfilling your promises and responsibilities across all areas of life.
- It shows that even if a relationship parts because it wasn't right for the adults, that they can still interact respectfully and politely

and that they don't have to argue, fight and seek revenge at the
expense of each other.

- The example from our new partners demonstrates that new,
complex, blended families can co-exist and adapt to
accommodate complex arrangements and be made to work for
the long term.

My greatest hope as a parent is to give my kids the best upbringing and
to teach them the lessons required to make them rounded human beings.
I want to give them the chance to live the happy and fulfilled life that I
live. While I hope for them that they will find a loving relationship and
never have to go through divorce, if they do so I hope that the lessons
their Mum and I (and their Step-Mum, Step-Dad and other adults around
them) have taught them by example, will help them to continue to adapt
and live happily.

I believe that nesting and co-parenting have been instrumental in helping
to impart these lessons to my kids and will help them to live the happy
lives I wish for them.

One place to call home

Home is where the heart is, and where I lay my head. I think it's a
valuable thing to never have to feel temporary about where you are.
Adaptability and flexibility are great skills to have, and I think my kids
have learned that they can be happy wherever they are in life as long as
they're safe and loved. Nonetheless while this flexibility has been
engendered in them through the co-parenting years, nesting has restored
for them a single place that they can call home at the end of each day.

They still stay at my new family home, have their own room there, and one at their Mum's new family home too. The nest has become their proper home though and I think this is a valuable thing for them in its own right.

For you as a divorced couple

Freedom of time to move on

A major side-effect for my ex and I, ever since we started co-parenting 50-50 has been that we have each been afforded approximately 50% of our life, free of childcare commitments or responsibility to rebuild our lives and move forwards. That's certainly not to say that I stop thinking about my kids when they're in her custody, or that I have nothing to do with them during those weeks; my eldest in particular tends to call me most days, and she also phones my parents, her grandparents most days too, to their considerable delight!

The reality though is that in most divorces, one parent usually ends up carrying the greater share of responsibility and time when they're caring for the kids. At the same time, the other parent likely yearns for more time with the kids. Co-parenting and nesting smooths this and balances it out a little more, particularly where it's a 50-50 split as we have. During this kids-free time, over the years I've been able to:

- Plan in and prioritise work-related travel, and schedule meetings that may take me away from home
- Socialise with friends without having to arrange child-care or babysitting

- Travel for leisure purposes where the trip wasn't suitable for my kids (such as to music festivals, one of my favourite hobbies)
- Return to the dating-scene once I'd worked through the healing from my divorce, to ultimately find a new partner and eventual wife
- Undertake home-improvement projects such as painting and decorating that wouldn't be made easier by the presence of kids!
- Relax, rest and recover from the rigours of looking after kids and catch up on sleep (when they were still young and prone to waking in the night).

These activities have all been universally made easier by having around half my life to plan them and undertake them guilt-free. The same benefit has been afforded to my ex and I believe that this has been a part of what has allowed us each to move forwards and give the kids our attention and regular, ongoing input for the many years since our divorce.

The guilt-free part has, admittedly, taken time to come to fruition, but this is part of the process of adapting and healing after divorce. It's inevitably hard at first to feel like you're putting your own needs to the fore, even if you're not doing this at the expense of your kids or their need of your time or focus.

Sense of co-operation

I doubt I'm unique in feeling that it's better to get on and have a life free of argument and acrimony. It's better to let go of past hurt and baggage than to carry it around, let it hamper you or define you. It's nice to be nice!

Co-parenting, and later nesting has allowed my ex and I to feel like we're operating in a spirit of co-operation and positivity rather than angst and tension. As I've mentioned before, we still have our differences of opinion and there'll be things that we never agree on. When it comes to daily life and functioning as a separated couple we're lucky to enjoy a sense of co-operation and calm.

I have no desire to be back in my marriage with her any more than she does with me. Equally I wish her no harm and know that a happy and fulfilled life for her will make her a happier person and ultimately a better Mum to our daughters. The co-parenting and nesting arrangement that we have maintained with a spirit of positivity and co-operation has been a big enabler to this from both sides. It's a good feeling to know that we're both being adult about things, and recognising that it's in our power to give the kids a good childhood, to put aside our differences where necessary, and to act with the kids' best interests at the fore.

An additional space to use when you have access to it
The last fringe-benefit of the nesting scenario is somewhat trivial, and may depend on the logistics of your arrangement. For us, since we both live in family homes an hour away from the nest, we have both benefitted at times from being able to use the nest as a further home when it was convenient to each other to do so. At times like summer-vacations and other public holidays we've occasionally been able to use the nest as a further family home, or just as a base for me and my wife when my ex was away with the kids. This has always been done openly and with each other's consent and it offers a benefit (particularly if, as is the case for us, the nest is located near a major city that we like visiting).

Financial Benefits

Nesting is by no-means a one-size-fits-all model for co-parenting after divorce and just as the financial constraints or challenges will depend on your circumstances, so too will the benefits you may receive from it. In the circumstances of my own divorce and separated family, you may recall that just prior to moving to a nesting model, my ex-wife and I had each established a new family home with our new spouses. These homes are each around an hour away in separate directions from the town in which we jointly raise our daughters from our failed marriage. To make co-parenting work, we were each also renting a home in that town which was only used for 50% of the time when the girls were living with each of us. The costs of these rentals along with associated utility costs, internet connection and so-on were all duplicate costs when you consider that the kids could only ever be with one of us at any one time. When we eventually consolidated to a single 'nest' then there were immediate financial benefits to us both in terms of saving expenditure and splitting costs that we'd both footed individually before.

Like I've said though, this is very specific to our circumstances.

Depending on what you read of the (currently very limited) literature on bird-nesting, you will find that the recommendations for when it is best used, can vary enormously. Some seem to favour nesting as a means of easing the transition for kids when a relationship fails. When you choose to employ it during the timeline of your divorce and life thereafter, will have some influence over the potential financial benefits can be realised.

Nesting when the relationship has just parted

If the parents, in their parting are able to contemplate nesting as the kids remain in the family home and each of the parents effectively moves out for a week at a time, then that could conceivably also offer a saving of money initially. Certainly, if each parent hasn't got to immediately secure a new home that is fit for them *and* the kids then there is a great deal more flexibility offered to them. The can each take on a lesser property for the times they're not in the nest as a stop-gap solution until such a time as they've each found their feet financially again. When the kid's needs are catered for as well as they were previously and the parent has only to find somewhere to live when they're not the resident parent, then there are a wider range of options available to them. They may be able to move in with friends or relatives, take a room in a shared house with other adults, or rent or purchase a small studio-apartment that has accommodation just for themselves.

In each of these scenarios the total cost of accommodation for each divorcing parent would presumably be more financially manageable than if each parent were individually trying to fund an entire family home themselves.

This is one very specific scenario in terms of the kids remaining in the family home. The same prospects for lessened accommodation costs and greater flexibility for the parents exists even if a new, slightly smaller and more befitting property is sourced to serve as the nest, from the outset.

Further financial benefits

With my experience after over ten years of parenting since divorce, I feel able to comment on a number of other areas where there are potential financial savings associated with nesting. Some of these are specific to nesting, but others apply more generally in relation to co-parenting which is naturally part of a nesting arrangement anyway.

It may be of use to you in considering the arrangement or in making it work so I have set these out below.

Accommodation costs – Not to labour the point, but looking only as far as the costs associated with providing the kids with the roof over their heads and the associated furniture, facilities and essentials of life, this is one area of great potential for saving money. If the kids are staying in one place, then there really only ever needs to be one set of costs associated with their upkeep. Of course, the divorcing or separating parents are each going to need to find somewhere else to live when not looking after the kids, but that's an inevitable part of splitting up. You're both presumably dedicated to a better way of raising your kids after divorce than is conventional, and are actively researching and considering co-parenting or even nesting. It stands to reason then that you'd both be willing to make sacrifices of your own short-term comfort if it were a means of ensuring that your kids have a comfortable home (which you also get to enjoy with them, for half the time!)

When the kids' needs are taken care of, I've found it far easier to compromise my own needs a little and use this as the source of inspiration to work harder, do better or earn more money as a means of improving my own life and then by definition, that of my kids too.

My advice then is to source a property to use as the nest which provides adequate, comfortable accommodation for the kids (but that isn't excessively big or expensive). You and your ex are then able to get something sorted for yourselves that gives you somewhere adequate to live in when you're not accompanying the kids as the live-in parent, until you're back on your feet again financially.

There may of course come a point where each of the adults moves on and finds a new partner or establishes a new family, either where your new partner has kids from a former relationship (as is the case for me) or where you end up having more kids with them. This will likely be hard to contemplate for you right now, just as it was for me, and I don't doubt that the idea of future relationships and dating is likely to be far from your mind. I've written a separate book on the subject of dating and relationships after divorce which you can access where you got hold of this one if you so wish.

The point is, eventually your personal situation and housing needs may well change. Eventually you may establish a new family home within which you may choose to establish a separate bedroom or space for your kids to use when they visit from the nest. Indeed, I'd recommend you do so to avoid your kids feeling excluded from the new home. This of course will represent a further cost, but for the context of this book I intend to focus only upon the essential costs of raising your kids and giving them the life they deserve. I thought it worth a mention though!

Food, utilities and facilities – There are the inevitable costs associated with keeping kids fed, watered and online these days that are of course equally important to them. For many kids, the thought of losing their internet connection seems sadly more important to them than food at times! The financial premise of the nesting model is that each of the parents contributes to the costs of the home equally, or at the very least in proportion to an arrangement that is fair to both parties. As such, it stands to reason that the apportionment of the costs of keeping the kids fed and of keeping the home warm, lit, clean and connected to the Internet will all be shared more equitably. We have also saved money by not paying for utilities and Internet connections in homes that are unoccupied for half the time.

We split the phone and internet bill between us, along with utilities and so-on. We each pay for one of the kids' cell-phone bills and it seems to work out evenly over time.

In terms of groceries, I shop for food that is eaten by me and the kids when I'm in the nest, and my ex does the same for when she's there. Inevitably there is a reduction in the wastage of food that may otherwise be brought about when excess milk, fruit and other perishables might otherwise be thrown away if not consumed when the kids were coming and going from one home to the other. This too offers a small saving towards the total costs for each of us.

Clothing, cosmetics and toiletries – Over the course of our co-parenting experience it became apparent that it wasn't desirable to duplicate on the purchase of all the various things that the girls needed, but in some cases we've had to do so anyway. This has applied to clothes and cosmetics, toys (when they were younger) and technology and gadgetry when they've grown older. It simply wasn't practical to have to move all their essentials back and forth between us from week to week. For this reason, when they were living between two homes there was an element of duplication of items that had to be paid for by each of us.

It made sense that they only had one set of school uniform, since they would generally transition between homes in the course of a school day (wearing the uniform) and could only ever be wearing it at school anyway. However, we each ended up paying for sets of clothes, underwear, basic toiletries and cosmetics and such to keep at each of our separate homes, the costs of which have undoubtedly mounted up over the years.

There were inevitably the favourite toys and garments that were still moved back and forth over the years; I think this is an essential concession to helping them to exist happily through the process. Once we moved to nesting, this immediately ceased to be a factor. The point is hopefully clear, but once they kids are in a single place there is no longer a need for them to have two sets of everything.

Chargers – One of the biggest challenges in co-parenting besides the more occasional serious stuff, has been the constant forgetting and misplacing of chargers required to keep phones, tablets and e-readers charged. These would routinely be left at one home or another, have to be retrieved, or on occasion they'd get lost or simply seem to evaporate in transit between homes! The number of replacements that have had to be purchased over time is significant and the number of frustrated car journeys necessitated to retrieve them from one home or another has been significant! I mention it with my tongue in cheek a little, but it's another issue that is negated by nesting (for the most part… things still get lost!). The chargers last a lot longer when they're rarely removed from the nest!

Comforters – In a similar vein to the charger issue, and depending on the age of your kids they may also have a favoured soft-toy, teddy bear or comforter that goes everywhere with them. When you have a single home that they tend to reside in, there's far less danger of these essential items being lost, left-behind or misplaced in transition between homes. I've also known families who tactically purchase a number of spare duplicates of such items and keep these in store. Depending on the cost of these, there lays another saving of money (and certainly of potential angst, heartache and sleepless nights when the item goes missing!)

Splitting of extraordinary costs – This book won't address all the financial aspects of divorce settlements, since it's an area of great complexity and one that's emotionally charged. The premise behind our divorced finances has always been that since we were equally funding the kids upbringing and equally contributing time and money to it, that we've always striven to each fund them for the time they were with us. I appreciate though that this is in part possible since we both earn a comparable income to each other.

Even if your finances require one or other of you to pay a regular maintenance allowance to the other under the terms of your divorce, the general premise that seems to work well in the context of co-parenting is that each of you funds the kids when they're living with you. The additional regular costs, like school uniform, shoes, fees for sports clubs, music lessons and so-on, we've always alternated who paid for them and monitored expenditure to keep things equitable. When one of us has bought one of the kids some school shoes, the next time the shoes in question need replacing the other of us will buy them. It keeps it fair and simple.

The other savings that have been facilitated by the nesting arrangement seem to be as a result of this ethos of things being shared or split equally as a general rule. We've always tried to split costs such as of school trips, equipment for sports and so-on, on an equal 50-50 basis as it's consistent with the overall financial terms of our split.

When the kids have needed computers and printers for homework, as seems to be an essential these days, then having a single printer, toner cartridges and paper at the nest seems to be more manageable an expense when you only have to restock every other time it runs out!

A side-effect rather than a purpose

The financial considerations are undoubtedly at the forefront of the minds of many who embark on divorce anyway, and the impacts of nesting do need to be evaluated to determine if it's viable for you. When you establish nesting, it needs to be sustainable and structured so that it will last, otherwise you risk further upheaval and upset in the future if it cannot be kept up.

The financial savings associated with nesting are certainly not presented here as a means for encouraging you to pursue it. As I've said, depending on how you set it up, the costs of it compared to other methods for managing your separated family may be greater. However, if you're both, as divorced parents, willing to adopt the ethos of co-operation and treating each other fairly and equitably then you can unlock certain small financial savings that might otherwise not be accessed, and this will undoubtedly help both of you as you move onwards in life.

It all comes down to your attitude to it!

Benefits as an individual

The best way of being a parent (after divorce)

A more significant benefit that I've felt as a result of first co-parenting my kids equally, and later as we've moved to nesting, is in genuinely feeling that this is the best possible way in which I can contribute to the upbringing of my kids. When my relationship with their mother failed, I was terrified of losing my place in their lives. Fortunately, we managed to find a way to make it work that meant we could both contribute to raising them and play an equally involved part in their lives. It's about more than a desire to split the custody and responsibility evenly, but also each being driven by having as much active input in the lives of the kids as we can.

In the heading for this section I've gone as far as putting *after divorce* into brackets, since at times I've even reflected that co-parenting, and later nesting, has enabled me to be a more hands-on, involved and effective parent than I feel I may have been within the context of my first marriage. Of course, this is completely theoretical and based on a subjective judgment. It's also purely my opinion.

My point though is that far from enabling an acceptable, but sub-standard parenting response to life after divorce, I think the model of parenting that we've used to raise our kids, separately but with equal input has given them a childhood that's been as supportive, loving and positive as any of their peers. It's not merely a case of getting-by and having made the best of a non-ideal or difficult situation, but of actually coming up with a model for raising our kids to live the best life possible, for them and for us individually too.

There have been many phases during the 10+ years since we divorced and inevitably my emotions have shifted a lot during that time. Early-on, the focus was upon healing and overcoming the inevitable emotional pain that accompanies divorce, even when it's an amicable split as ours was. Later, the focus of my mind shifted to the possibility of a new start to life, the opportunity to shape it as I wanted, and eventually also to the possibility of a new relationship. I've dated and eventually remarried (and in-between, even been engaged again to someone else. It's an ill-fated tale that you can read more about in my book on dating and relationships if you're sufficiently intrigued; it was messy!). Throughout all these phases, I've remained resolved to be the best parent I could to my kids. I wasn't content for them to suffer or receive a sub-standard childhood as a result of mine and their Mum's inability to form a lasting relationship.

I'm now remarried with two step-kids from my second wife's first marriage, and a blended family of six of us when we're all together. At one stage we did consider moving her kids to the school system where my girls are established, and all living full-time in one home (with my girls coming and going for their alternate week). In the end we rejected this idea, both as we didn't want to introduce further upheaval for her kids in moving schools, but also because nesting for mine seemed like the better option for them.

There was also the added dynamic that we weren't sure how a full-time sharing of me as their father, would work for mine in not having me to themselves. This isn't to say that we couldn't have made it work if it were the only option available to us. I suppose it's more the case that without certainty over how well such a set-up could work for all involved, it wasn't something that we felt strongly about putting in place as an experiment with a risk of failure.

This brings up a further point that I want to emphasize. No matter where you are within the timeline of your life during or after divorce, you will undoubtedly have a sense of 'this is it' about where you are now and it being the state in which you and your kids will exist forever more. I can offer you the reassurance not only that things will change over time (for this is an inevitability). It will also be the case that the situation will change for the better and improve as long as you strive for it to do so.

Critical to remember throughout this time in your life and onwards, is that you should accept and expect that you will need to allow the parenting model for your kids to change and evolve too. I'm not saying that you should be chopping and changing it on a whim, and I've already explored the importance that I see in maintaining structure and stability. However, over time you will move on from your failed marriage, likely change jobs, move house, potentially have new relationships, careers and maybe even more kids. So too will your ex! All these events will have potential impacts on how you raise your kids and the arrangements you put in place for their upbringing. It's essential to be open and receptive to this change and to consider that what works now, may not work in the future. As long as you're basing decisions on what is best for the kids (in line with my golden rule number 1) then you will be coming from the right place.

My daughters are now teenagers, and the eldest will soon leave home for university. They value their time with each of their Mum and I. It seems to me that each week they have the undivided time and attention of either their Mum or I (shared with their sibling of course). When I'm the live-in parent, it's just me and the girls which is a setup that they've become accustomed to for most of their living memory. When my ex is the parent of the week, they have her to themselves too. As a result of this, I believe that both my ex and I each have a much stronger individual bond with both of our kids than we might otherwise have enjoyed if they'd grown up in a conventional non-separated family, and certainly in a more conventional separated family.

When I'm with the girls, naturally I miss my second-wife and step-kids but I find that my focus is freed to look after the girls and meet their needs. I'm on hand with undivided attention to help them as they need me to, I cook for them (not because I feel obliged to, but because I want to give them the best possible support I can as they manage the demands of full-time education). I'm able to spend time enjoying their company and to do things together and apart during our free time with them that I might otherwise not be able to if there were also younger kids around, or even if both parents were in the same home. We go out to play sports together, we attend concerts, watch movies and generally enjoy being around each other. They also have the freedom to enjoy their free time, as do I. I don't want to give the impression that my kids are spoilt and demanding of attention as I don't feel this is the case. I focus on them, and do what I want to do for them, but I also respect their independence and they do the same for me.

I think that this is also a factor in making it easier for them to accept that for the time I'm not with them, I'm with my wife and the step-kids. I can imagine if there were a sense that someone else's kids were getting more of my time, attention and resources than they were, there might be cause for some jealousy or resentment. As it is, I think that this has been kept to a minimum for the fact that they have me to themselves for half the time. I can assure you that jealousy and step-sibling rivalry still comes up from time-to-time. I suspect though that it's far less prevalent than it could be in our family. I credit the opportunities enabled by the nesting arrangement with that reduction.

The impacts on future partners is considered separately in this book but I want to touch upon it in this context too. My co-parenting arrangement and the need to be in the same place as my girls for alternate weeks was a pre-existing requirement when I met my second wife. She has known this about me since we met and I hope and believe that she accepts and respects this about me and my life. I also believe the arrangement benefits her and her kids (my step-kids) too as they get time together as the three of them. They were a unit before we got married, without me on the scene. This balances out the time when I'm there on alternate weeks as live-in husband and Step-Dad. The intricacies of our arrangement are likely to be different to yours, but I emphasize this to point out that with an open mind and an optimistic outlook, many situations that are challenging on first sight, can be made to work and offer benefit.

As ever, when trying to forecast how others see the situation, it's quite hard to know if you've got it right. I do have a good sense though that through the open and honest communication we have between us all, that it's been possible to genuinely seek and be given the opinions of our kids on how the arrangements work for all of them too. As such, there is more than a little feedback that has been received 'from the horse's mouth' as it were! The same is true in regard to the opinions of my wife on the arrangement.

I don't want to give the impression that this arrangement is easy at all times, in terms of being away from my wife. However, as a pre-existing condition when we met, it's just been something that we have naturally incorporated into our lives and which we manage and accept. It's not ideal at times, but we make it work.

I think this is a really good illustration of the ethos that has to be adopted when building a new family life and structure after divorce. Nothing is what could be rationally be described as *ideal* since it doesn't conform to conventional standards. There is no one-size-fits-all model for a separated family (or even for a non-separated family). For some reason, it seems that after divorce the arrangement that is most commonly put in place, what most people tend to resort to, is something that isn't really designed around what would be in the best interests of *most* of the affected parties.

When you consider how *most* of the people in the arrangement can get what *most* of them want, *most* of the time, your attention focuses on an arrangement that may not be ideal for anyone but which ticks *most* of the boxes. This is the essence of compromise generally, and I think that nesting illustrates where we've demonstrated the ability to do this well, for all our benefits.

Let's look at some of the other benefits that arise out of nesting when it's done well.

Time for myself

This has been another benefit consistent between the time when we were practising conventional co-parenting and now, as we practice bird-nesting. Many of those who are critical of co-parenting feel that it can be detrimental for kids to switch back and forth between parents who equally contribute to their upbringing. This seems to be due to the uncertainty and constant change that they perceive that it brings to life for the kids. I personally feel that the opposite is true. It offers structure, continuity and ensures that the kids benefit from the ongoing and continued input and involvement from both parents. It also teaches the kids the importance of self-reliance and being flexible and accepting change and the need for adaptability in their lives.

Without wanting to sound too self-congratulatory, in spite of divorce I feel that I've been as present in the lives of my kids, if not more present than I would have been had we not divorced. I also feel that I've played more active a role in their upbringing than I might otherwise have done in a non-separated family.

With that said, one significant benefit that has arisen from the co-parenting and subsequent bird-nesting arrangements for me has been in the free time that it has afforded me in my life since me and my ex parted.

When we first split up and at all times since, I definitely miss the girls when I'm not around them; please don't believe that I'm cold-hearted about it! However, I've come to grow accustomed to the fact that I spend around half of my life apart from them, and I'm sure they feel the same way regarding me and their Mum. A side-effect of the arrangement is that this has afforded me more personal space in my life when I'm not with the girls. At first this was invaluably useful in giving me time and space to work through the pain and hurt from parting and to adapt to life after divorce. In the years since, this has then become time that was useful for building my new life, career, eventually dating, forming new relationships and finally in establishing a new marriage. The most crucial aspect of this free time is that it has come available while being entirely free of guilt (or at least free of any just-cause to feel guilt; like most well-meaning humans I can't help but feel guilty from time to time)!

I've never had to bargain away my time spent alone, arrange baby-sitters, call in favours or feel guilty for neglecting the kids or making the most of the time when they were with me. I've just become adept at using the time when they weren't with me for anything that was better-pursued when I had my 'kids-free' time. This is of course my choice in terms of how I manage my commitments to the kids and how I plan my time when they've been with their Mum. There is no right or wrong way and I know that the kids would be happy in the past to have a baby-sitter occasionally if there were things I needed or wanted to do of an evening when they were with me. The general principle has been though that I've compartmentalised my life to be more focused on them when they were with me.

You may say that other divorced parents who have a conventional split would have free time too, particularly a parent who has less custody than the primary carer. I'd contend though that for most parents who actually yearn to play a significant part in the raising of their kids, this time would unavoidably come at a cost of guilt and yearning for the kids. That's not to say they *should* feel guilty for pursuing their own happiness or using their time effectively. I suspect though that for many, the guilt comes along with the time away from their kids, especially if they can't get as much access to their kids as they would like.

I'm being very careful about how I try and emphasise this point in terms of my own life and how I feel. Essentially it comes down to my conscience being clear for knowing that I've never walked away from responsibility as far as my kids and I know that they're well taken care of when they aren't with me. Indeed, I've actually sought responsibility out, actively chosen to raise them jointly with my ex, and I've delivered on it with as much conviction and commitment as possible. I've deliberately gone out to be as actively involved in my kids' upbringing as possible, effectively adopting the role of part-time single-parent for 50% of my life for the last 10+ years. As a result of this, I feel justified in accepting the benefit of the time when I don't have the girls as having been used as my own, to reclaim and build my new life.

My satisfaction in this is further warranted since I don't walk away from the girls when they're not my responsibility feeling like I've 'done my bit' regardless of the circumstances they're living in for the rest of the time. I am pretty certain that their mother feels the same way, and justifiably so. I don't ignore texts or calls from them when they're on their mothers' watch. I attend school concerts, meetings, sporting events and other commitments even if they don't fall in my week. The point is, in adopting a child-centric approach I fulfil on my commitments to them, but allow myself to live my own life to the full as well.

We've both committed to be active in their upbringing and will remain committed to this for life, alongside furthering our own lives outside of the parenting roles we both fulfil.

Undoubtedly some will dispute this as a benefit and maybe even criticise me for even venturing this as a viewpoint. I simply don't see why this is a problem though! Me and my ex-wife have absolutely put the interests of our kids to the fore since the day we split. Our relationship as a couple failed, but our relationship as parents to the kids is for all-time. As such, we've put in place a structure that we felt was the best way of raising them with equal active involvement. A natural side-effect of this structure (which has evolved over time as as the needs of our kids has changed) is that we have each been given around half of our lives freed from the immediate role of parent in residence to the girls. This has served us both well in allowing us to rebuild our lives and find new, happy relationships.

This in turn has also served (speaking only for myself) to make me happier as a person and happier as a parent as a result of this.

Depending on your viewpoint, you will have your own opinion on whether I'm unreasonable in this. I'm sure that as time goes on you will form your own opinions and face judgement from others arising from theirs about how kids of divorce should be raised. All I ask is that you bear in mind that the time it frees up to pursue your own life, *guilt free*, is one significant benefit of co-parenting and bird-nesting.

Again, it shouldn't be stated as your main aim from nesting, but certainly it's one benefit to keep in mind!

Chapter Six -
The Challenges

Having discussed the many benefits that arise from the arrangement, many of which are common to both co-parenting and bird-nesting, it seems sensible to consider some of the challenges arising from the arrangement.

My purpose in this book is not to *sell* you on the idea of bird-nesting or indeed co-parenting at any cost, or to portray it as a solution or structure that will work for all separated families; it simply won't work for everyone. Hopefully by now you are forming an idea of whether it could work for you and your kids. My goal is to present you with a balanced perspective on all the pre-requisites and considerations as well as both the good and bad sides in order that you can make an objective judgement as to whether it will work for you.

To re-emphasise, while you may reach the conclusion that it isn't right for you *right now*, I whole-heartedly recommend that you remain open-minded to it for the future. A childhood is a long time, and the needs of your kids and your circumstances and mind-set will undoubtedly change over the years following your divorce. Just because it seems unappealing or impossible to establish right now, one day it could become appealing or viable. Maintain an open mind!

By now you're hopefully thinking about whether the arrangement could work for you, and are starting to understand how it works and what benefits it could enable for your kids, you and your ex. How about the challenges and difficulties though? Undoubtedly there are many potential pitfalls to be aware of and I'll lay these out for you now.

I don't want to treat this as a list of insurmountable challenges since I believe that in life, with the right attitude and determination to overcome obstacles, most things can be dealt with if your motive to do something is strong enough. If obstacles are treated as part of the process of learning, rather than something that blocks the path, then I find that I learn, grow and achieve far more than if I allow myself to be defeated or have my course changed by factors outside of my control. How you approach these will determine if they put you off nesting or whether you foresee aspects of the arrangement that will be more challenging and stretching, but which you can still work around.

The challenges I highlight below then are more a series of lessons learned to-date, that should be considered if you are either interested in establishing nesting, or are looking for reassurance that challenges you're already facing in making it work, are common to all who have used the structure. Sometimes, when you're facing a problem or difficulty it can be helpful to know that others are going through or have been through the same!

Financial challenges

Inevitably one of the first of these challenges arises from the financial aspect of nesting. In common with the earlier discussion of the financial benefits of nesting, the challenges also arise depending on the individual circumstances and choices you make. Whether the situation is financially challenging or beneficial is determined to a large extent upon how you as a divorced or separated couple approach it. Factors such as the cost of housing in the location within which you live will be relevant to this. If your separated family is intending to reside in central London or New York City, then your living costs will be radically greater than if you want to live in the rural Mid-West USA or Central England.

Most fundamentally the costs of housing you, your kids and your ex will determine the level of challenge that the finances may present. The choices that you and your ex make about how you meet yours and your kids' housing needs will determine the overall cost.

At this point it may be worth reading back over the logic in the corresponding financial benefits section of this book to remind yourself of how the numbers can prospectively stack-up. If each parent could potentially secure some low-cost accommodation for use when they don't have the kids (such as a studio apartment or even a room in a house-share), with the costliest home being the 'nest', then the costs of housing are likely to be as manageable as they can possibly be in the context of life after divorce.

If, alternatively, one or both of you have greater aspirations and each feel that you need (or deserve) a bigger home or apartment to live-in, in addition to the nest, then of course the financial aspect to your nesting arrangement will be more stretching. I'm not judging this as a choice, and it really comes down to priorities and preferences as well as any specific needs that each of you has. It's worth thinking in the first instance though of minimizing your requirements personally when you're not in the nest, and seeking more modest housing in the first instance. That financial sacrifice on your part may help you to test whether the arrangement might work for you all, or not. It will certainly allow you to get your life post-divorce in better order, more quickly.

It could be that the area or country in which you live has districts that would be unsafe or unappealing to live in and hence the cost of your accommodation in addition to the nest becomes greater than it may ideally be, as you all deserve to feel safe and secure. One or other (or both) of you may have special housing needs, for adaptations or facilities made necessary by a particular medical condition, that makes securing low-cost accommodation more difficult. In short, there are a vast array of theoretical scenarios that could apply in different circumstances. It all depends on your needs and your choices!

The distinction should be made though, between what each of you *needs* versus what each of you *wants*. If you set out looking for a home when you're not living in the nest, and you feel entitled to a penthouse apartment with sea-views, then I'm presuming you have the money to afford this in addition to ensuring that your nest is suitably appointed. Presumably in this scenario, your ex may have similar tastes and expectations too. The establishment of your new homes cannot be allowed to become a competition that detracts from the co-operation that should be embedded and inherent within the arrangement.

Remember that the very premise of nesting (calling to memory the golden rules introduced at the start of the book) is that the needs and requirements of the kids comes first. As such, if the nest caters adequately for their needs, I'd contend that most parents are able to make some compromises when it comes to the level of luxury they need for themselves individually, at least until they are back on their feet.

Another factor that will contribute to the costs of housing is dependent on *when* you put the arrangement in place. Many articles on the subject suggest it as a good means of transitioning out of the marriage. The theory seems to go that on divorcing, the kids remain in the former family home and the parents come and go, securing other places to live in addition to the former family home. I've discussed the relative merits and drawbacks of this approach elsewhere in the book. In the context of finances, it would be reasonable to assume that the costs of this home are going to remain, somehow split between the divorcing couple (ideally 50-50) and that each will then be responsible for finding some new, additional accommodation. In this sense and following the logic through, the total housing costs are inevitably going to go up when combined together, as each shares the cost of the nest and an additional home. That said, the degree to which this will increase is all down to the size and standard of accommodation that each secures in addition to the nest.

In the context of nesting, housing costs post-divorce will account for a greater proportion of your combined income than if you each funded half of the family home pre-divorce (as you will each have to pay something towards another property too). However, the combined costs won't necessarily be greater than if you were both funding a separate family home and having the kids half the time. This is simply illustrated by the below examples, using some contrived and simple examples with round numbers. The logic is sound though and based on my own experience of life since divorce:

Married Family of 4 in a 3 bedroomed house:

Rent = £900 per month

Divorced Couple with the same 3 bedroomed house, splitting rent 50-50 and each securing a separate 1 bed studio apartment:

Combined rent:

3 bedroomed house = £900 Per month

Studio 1 = £450 per month

Studio 2 = £450 per month

Total rent = £1800 per month

Individual share = £900 per month

Divorced couple with 2 separate 3 bedroomed houses, each paying for their own property

3 bedroomed house number 1 = £900 Per month

3 bedroomed house number 2 = £900 Per month

Total rent = £1800 per month

Individual share = £900 per month

I realise that these are conveniently round numbers but I haven't tried to present an overly optimistic view of the situation, I promise! These are the relative costs of property in many areas close to where I live and I use them to emphasise a point; depending on the choice of property, nesting *doesn't have to be costlier* than funding the housing required for conventional co-parenting, if the property is chosen appropriately.

This of course represents a best-case. When you factor in the additional bills and other costs associated with multiple properties (such as gas, electricity, water, telephone, Internet, cable service and property taxes) then there is a real chance that the combined cost of properties is going to increase in both cases, regardless of whether you are considering nesting, co-parenting from separate properties or any other model of separated parenting.

If you are committed to find a way of putting your kids' needs to the fore when working out the logistics of your divorce, then undoubtedly compromises will need to be made by both parents. I assume that as you've gone as far as considering this approach then you are committed to this principle, and as such the financial challenges simply need to be explored and worked around. All of this is a long-form way of saying that it doesn't *have to be* more expensive than co-parenting, or a barrier to considering it or making it work. If your intent and desire to make nesting or co-parenting work for the kids is strong enough, there are always ways around the financial challenges.

Closer proximity to your Ex

One of the biggest tests presented by nesting as a whole is that there is a much closer visibility afforded into the details of your ex's life. Your individual circumstances and the intricacies of your relationship with your ex will determine how much of an issue or challenge this presents.

The same is true (to an extent) when co-parenting on a 50-50 basis in that you will be regularly passing the kids between yourselves. A weekly interaction became the norm for us for many years while our standard co-parenting was in place, on handover day.

Again, when putting the needs of the kids to the fore, this becomes something else that you have to work around and accept as part of the arrangement that you have to deal with if you are to make it work. The premise is that since you are divorcing or divorced, you must have had significant enough difficulties and differences of opinion to force you to part, so it's a given that this is going to be somewhat uncomfortable and require some compromise on both parts.

Acting with respect and basic good manners is often all that's required to make the interactions relatively peaceful and polite, at least on a superficial level, which is all the kids really need from you anyway.

In my experience
When we used to co-parent our kids from two separate properties, we actually had more interaction and direct face-to-face contact with each

other than we do now. The arrangement used to be such that we'd switch the kids over from one property to another on a Monday. On a Monday morning, the kids would be dropped off at school by the parent who had-had custody of them for the previous 7 days, and they'd be picked up from school by the other parent on Monday evening. There would usually be a need for some of their possessions (clothes, toys and so-on) to be picked up from the home where they'd been for the previous week.

If the kids were transiting to me I would generally take them round to their Mums to fetch the bags that they would (hopefully) have packed at some point over the weekend towards the end of their time at their Mums. More often they wouldn't have packed in advance, and so would be scurrying around and gathering the things they felt were essential to bring for the next week at mine. Depending on how long this took, my ex and I would usually have a quick chat while the kids gathered their stuff to bring to mine, mostly just to figure out logistics and anything else that needed to be covered between us in the coming week, such as school meetings, trips, homework assignments, sports clubs and so-on. After that, the kids would say their farewells to their Mum for a week and off we'd go. The same process would follow in reverse at the end of the next week when the same bags would be filled with the same essential possessions in readiness to be shifted back to their Mum's home.

Whilst I would generally feel a little frustrated at the kids repeatedly not getting their stuff together on a Sunday night in order that we could just call-by to pick up a ready-packed bag, I used to find this handover process quite useful. I've since realised that my desire for them to be packed and ready was more a reflection of my love for preparation and order than a genuine expectation that I ever thought would be met.

We have always tried to avoid making kids the messenger or go-between to pass messages and information between us; it seems unfair in the circumstances and is merely passing the buck onto them when the divorced parents are unwilling or unable to be co-operative and communicative with each other. To this end, it was always handy to have a quick face to face chat with my ex to quickly discuss the things that needed to be discussed, either with the kids present or behind closed doors if appropriate. It also meant we could hand over things that needed to be exchanged for the week, such as letters from school, medicines, or anything else that needed to come with the girls. If we had a list of things to cover, I saw no harm in jotting down a note for myself to ensure that I covered everything that needed to be discussed. I could then leave my ex alone for the week, and enjoy the kids for the week while they were with me.

I realise that the circumstances of your split will determine whether you think this will be helpful, terrifying or an aggravation that you would rather avoid. All I can say is to remind you that with the purpose of co-parenting and nesting being to put the kids first, a regular and fluid exchange of information between you and your ex is essential. As such you do need to have a means of regular communication between you, if only in regard to the kids. A once a week meeting informally, helps make this possible.

Since we've moved to nesting, this interaction in person has become almost non-existent. On a Monday, she might see the girls off to school, and at some point after she will tidy the apartment, and head off to work. I will arrive at some point later in the day and move in. By the time the kids finish at school, I'm installed and settled in as parent for the week. I've described this in detail to point out that in reality we have very little direct, in-person interaction unless we arrange to meet. We will often communicate by email, text or phone if there's something child-related we need to discuss, but months can pass when we don't see each other in person.

Depending on the age of your kids it might be that the above model doesn't apply for you. If your kids were younger than school age for example, of course they'd need to be handed over from one to the other. For older kids though, I don't believe that a face-to-face handover would be necessary with the nest being used as the base for the kids regardless of which parent was in residence.

Challenges for yourself

Having described how there's no need for physical interaction, I appreciate that this isn't the main area of conceptual challenge for those who contemplate nesting. In the earlier description of the ins and outs of how the nest is set up, you'll recall that we go to great lengths to ensure that the nest is treated as the kids' home and we're the guests. Neither of us leaves our stuff laying around, there isn't a great deal of personalisation of the nest to make it either mine or hers. Even having gone to these lengths there are inevitably still signs of her having been in the apartment just as there are of my presence when she moves in.

What needs to be accepted by divorced parents considering bird-nesting is that they *will* have to deal with a greater degree of visibility into the life of their ex than they might like, or otherwise have in a conventional set-up. It's down to each of you to manage this, to maintain healthy barriers for your own sanity and out of respect for the other person's privacy.

For the purposes of disclosure, I've outlined all the possible ways in which this challenge could arise, but not all of them are things that I've had to deal with relating to my ex. They are just the areas of difficulty that I could see potentially arising!

Fighting for space in the fridge and cupboards – This is an annoyance that I suffer, but only as it represents the first thing that I have to do each week when I arrive at the nest. I tend to arrive having visited the supermarket on the way, with food for the week. I'm immediately confronted with a fridge that is likely to contain the leftovers or near-empty packages of food that my ex has provided for her week. Dealing with this, throwing out food that has gone out of date, reorganising the contents of the fridge so that her food is in one area and putting mine away takes just a few minutes. While this all probably makes me sound petty, you can hopefully see where this represents a modest annoyance if only as part of the process of moving in for another week. It's no worse than the challenge that many face when putting away food after a trip to the supermarket, but I appreciate for some that this could be a source of annoyance when the inconvenience can be attributed to their ex-wife or husband.

Dealing with reminders of their presence – While we've gone out of our way not to personalise the nest to our individual tastes, there will be things that still stand out as theirs and yours. It's an inevitability. I see numerous signs of her presence around the place, and reminders of her habits, just as I'm sure she sees similar markers of my own. Things as simple as little ways that furniture may be rearranged in the course of their week, books left lying around and so-on can all act as reminders that they've been there. It's not a rational reaction to have to such trivial things. If it used to annoy you that your ex would lay in the bath reading, and afterwards leave piles of crumpled and discarded magazines on the bathroom floor when you were together, then chances are the discarded magazines are still going to annoy you now. Such things may be trivial, but in the context of doing the best by your kids after divorce, hopefully the corrosive effects of such things can be minimised and kept in perspective.

Clearing up their mess – Maybe they've had to leave in a hurry and not cleaned the bathroom. Perhaps they've forgotten to hoover the bedroom before leaving. It could be that they left the dishwasher half-full of dishes and hadn't run it because it was half-full. Maybe they left it full of clean dishes and you have to empty it, taking five precious minutes out of your day to do a chore that was theirs by-rights? No matter how much the bird-nesting model is a means of equipping you and your ex with a hotel-like facility for parenting, in reality you are unlikely to have a butler or maid who can make the transition between you seamless. There will always be things that one or other of you forgets to do or take care of before moving out for the week. This is unavoidable. What matters most is the intent to be as efficient and rigorous as you each can be in making the place presentable and clean for your ex to arrive. For some this will be a matter of pride, for others it will be done begrudgingly. Nonetheless, there's a need for it to be done, and to be done with as good and positive a spirit as possible. It all comes back to making a home that is clean, comfortable and which runs smoothly for the ultimate benefit of your kids.

Accepting damage caused by them – Accidents happen and things get broken. How will you feel if your favourite coffee-cup gets accidentally smashed when they were in the nest? What if an item of furniture breaks just as they are moving out for the week and you have to co-ordinate with the landlord to get it fixed? Maybe the water-heater will break and you somehow consider it their fault since it happened on their watch? All of these are trivial events that happen regularly in any household. Pinning it on your ex, even if there was some cause-and-effect, and especially if there wasn't, is utterly futile.

Unblocking the sink from their waste – Nobody likes unblocking the sink of food-waste, or having to pull clumps of hair out of the shower drain when it refuses to drain. How will you feel knowing that it's your ex's hair contributing to the blockage? Why haven't they dealt with it themselves? Nobody is immune from having to do such unpleasant domestic tasks and there's little point in adding to your frustrations by considering the cause as being somehow your ex's fault. Maybe it's your hair or food waste causing the blockage!

Reminders of their shopping habits – Through food in the fridge, cleaning products in the bathroom and branded carrier bags left around the apartment you will become painfully aware of the ways in which they spend their money. You may prefer bulk-buying at a wholesaler to save money (indeed the terms of your divorce may require that you do) whereas you'll see signs that they shop for premium brands at a high-end supermarket. Whether this was a lasting frustration or dissatisfaction from your marriage, or whether it's a frustration that has come about since divorce, you'll have visibility of it and will have to deal with it. Judging and feeling angry about it will be futile.

Dealing with their habits and mannerisms – Your ex may have been a slob, or a clean-freak. You will have to each sign up (metaphorically) to a collective understanding that you'll each do your best to tidy up the nest before you hand it over to the other, but invariably their standards of cleanliness and tidiness may not meet yours. Alternatively, you may find their expectations constraining and restrictive. Either way, these probably serve as reminders of some the annoyances you felt when you were deciding to part.

It's essential to find ways of not letting such minor things get to you and to treat the annoyance as nothing more than a minor and momentary difficulty rather than a cause for a long-term grievance.

Rounding up

The fundamental basis of the bird-nesting approach is to put the kids needs to the fore. They don't care if you get annoyed that there's a bit of food accidentally left on the kitchen worktop by your ex that needs to be wiped up. The kids don't care that this may have been a repeated annoyance when you were still married that your ex couldn't proactively clean up after themselves. The kids aren't concerned that you have to juggle food around a bit between shelves in the fridge to make space for your groceries. They're understandably disinterested if you get annoyed that the radio has been tuned to a different station from the one you prefer.

The fundamental skill to master for nesting is a willingness to compromise and to deal with minor-annoyances in the interests of the greater good; giving your kids a happy, fulfilled and loving childhood with the active involvement of both parents!

Challenges for the kids

With the fundamental mantra and purpose of nesting now hopefully becoming apparent to you (if it wasn't already), you may not be surprised to note that even though the nesting arrangement is child-centric, it's still a challenge at times to cater to their whims and needs, and to make them completely happy. The challenges for the kids in relation to nesting are more fundamental than whether Mum buys their favourite brand of orange juice or whether Dad lets them watch TV while they eat dinner. The challenges for kids that I've observed stem from adapting to what is undoubtedly an unusual way of life.

As you will appreciate as a parent, kids are always comparing their lives to those of their friends and peer-group. Unfortunately, it's not that unusual nowadays to be a child of divorce, but a child whose parents co-parent equally is still a relative novelty in the UK at least. I've no statistics to back this up other than experience in observing my own kids and their friends. I'm not aware of *any* of their friends whose parents are divorced or separated who have been raised 50-50 by the two parents, let alone any who have adopted nesting.

I've outlined the challenges that I can foresee would emerge for kids in a nesting arrangement. Again, some of these are derived from experience and others based on things I've read but they represent some of the things to anticipate and consider.

Confusion over their parents' relationship with each other

In my opinion this is most likely to arise when the kids are younger and in particular when the pre-divorce family home is used as the nest. When the kids are potentially struggling to understand what it means for their parents to be splitting up, and trying to accept that there will be changes in how their family works, it would of course seem confusing that they will remain living in the same place, and with both their parents coming and going and looking after them in the same home.

The clear differentiator is hopefully apparent in that there will never be a time (other than in passing) where both the parents are there at the same time and this in itself should help the kids understand. There is however a school of thought that in preserving such a proportion of pre-divorce life that the kids cling onto a hope that their parents may eventually resolve their differences and get back together. I'm assuming this isn't your intention as you enter into nesting.

The resolution to this scenario is, I suppose, to try and ensure a clarity and consistency of message for the kids regarding the true fate of the relationship from the outset of divorce and throughout their lives. Whether bird-nesting is a means of softening the blow of transitioning through divorce, or whether it's a long-term measure, the kids still need to be clear that it's a means of them remaining in the home, and with regular 'separate but together' input from both their parents.

For our kids, this was never a factor. As I've previously mentioned, they are unlikely to have living memory of me and their Mum ever being together and have grown up knowing that we weren't together and would never be together. Throughout this time, we've shown that while we have our differences, we still respect each other, are able to communicate effectively with each other, and are equally committed to being there for the girls no matter what direction our lives take.

When we moved to nesting, when the girls were both teenagers it was easy to position the move as a positive for them (as well as for us). What was also important was that we portrayed it as something of a living experiment to begin with. We all reserved the right to revert back to our previous arrangements if it ever ceased to work well for us all. I suppose to an extent we all still reserve that right even now. There was a significant part of the move to nesting which was intended to address dissatisfactions that both the girls had voiced, namely that they were fed-up with moving back and forth. As such, it was an easy-sell to get them interested in the idea when their Mum first came up with it.

I guess that fundamental to overcoming any confusion for the kids is that their understanding and interpretation is always going to be driven first and foremost by the things they see and hear and the behaviours that they observe from their parents, two of their most important role-models.

There will only be cause for confusion if you give them cause for confusion. It will be clear to them if you're just using this as a means of maintaining a 'friends-with-benefits' relationship just as much as if you're using this as a means of delaying the blow of a full-fledged divorce since you think you're being kind to them by slowly dismantling the relationship. Bear this in mind when you're establishing bird-nesting and as you live with the arrangement since perception is the biggest part of reality. In my experience, kids are extremely perceptive and are often able to deduce and understand more than many adults give them credit for.

Adapting to two different sets of rules

In my books on co-parenting I go to lengths to emphasise the importance of both parents having a joint vision for how they want the kids to be raised, as well as sharing a common ethos and expectations of behaviour and discipline in their kids. Individual house-rules will vary and there will undoubtedly be one parent who is stricter, one who is pickier about tidiness, one who lets them get away with more, and one who lets them eat dinner on the couch. Such things are less important if the same overriding principles of behaviour, diligence and conduct apply regardless of which parent is in charge.

When we were co-parenting from two separate homes I was aware of different expectations and rules in each home. It always stunned and impressed me just how easily the girls would transition and adapt to each home. I recall describing in a previous book how I once had cause to observe the girls' routine for getting ready for school in their Mum's home compared to mine. The differences were staggering. In my home it was very regimented and I'd do a lot for them (such as laying out their uniform, making their breakfast and so-on). In their Mum's home it was chaotic but they did everything themselves and were still ready for school, well-presented, and on-time.

I think on reflection that their Mum had it right!

We're talking here of what most would consider fairly minor rules and expectations, things such as whether kids are expected to turn out their dirty laundry rather than leaving it in a pile on their bedroom floor, whether they have to wash dishes, put away their toys and so-on. These are potentially trivial things to most, but if the parents have differences of opinion and expectation from the kids in regard to how they're done, then there will be a source of potential challenge when all living under the same roof, albeit at different times.

Differences existed between how the two households ran and they still do. I believe that part of what made it easy for the girls to shift between the two sets of rules was in physically moving from one home to the other and mentally making the shift as part of the move. I don't doubt that in moving to the nest we've somehow made it more difficult for the girls to adapt each week. I still arrive on a Monday night with my expectations of how things will run for the week, and the following Monday their Mum arrives and her rules apply. Inevitably as the kids get older and approach adulthood we're all a bit more flexible and able to adapt and compromise, but I suspect that this will be a factor for the remainder of their childhoods nonetheless.

If you and your ex have differing approaches to the fundamentals of how daily life is run 'on your watch' then it will either be your responsibility to adapt your expectations, or the kids will have to adapt each week. Bear in mind that when they're remaining in one home and the rules are effectively changing around them, then this will of course have implications and potentially represent a challenge for them.

Wanting a dog

One final area of challenge that I want to address, I've flippantly noted under the heading of *wanting a dog*. The unfulfilled desire for a pet dog on the part of my kids has been one aspect of life for one of my daughters that brings her the most ongoing disappointment in life and resentment towards me! She is desperate to have a dog. While we've gone to lengths to try and accommodate the most important aspects of continuity and consistency in our parenting, and have done what we could to make the kids happy this is one area that still eludes me.

My ex would probably have a dog (certainly of the two of us she's the one more likely to entertain the idea at least), and my daughter would be delighted. Since we've moved to bird-nesting this is finally a feasible means of my daughter having the pet that she's so desperate for (in her mind). The challenge is that I have absolutely no desire to have a dog. I don't see our nest as being compatible with dog ownership (a second-floor apartment with no garden, which gets very hot in summer!).

The conclusion for my daughter is that I'm the blocker to her getting what she wants, albeit that this is a concession that relies too heavily on our nesting arrangement and would take it too far towards being a non-separated family structure, in my opinion. I hope you can see the subtle distinction. For me, the goal of the nesting arrangement isn't to live as closely as possible to being a non-separated family but without me and her Mum ever seeing each other. No amount of her complaining about how unfair it is will make a difference. We are both committed to giving her and her sister the best childhood we can with us both present, but we have to draw the line at it being used as a means of getting anything and everything that she would want.

She'll have to make do with a goldfish for now and get a dog when she leaves home!

Such considerations and challenges are likely to be relatively few in the context of nesting. I mention it mainly since such challenges are prone to arise when the more fundamental and day-to-day issues (the bigger things) have been ironed-out. They're worth being mindful of though.

Rounding up

There are undoubtedly a range of challenges for kids that arise from nesting. As I hope you can see, with sensitive and consistent handling I believe that the challenges and potential drawbacks are negligible for the kids when compared to the quality of life that it enables. The kids are able to have the consistent and regular involvement of both their parents in their life, with the freedom to remain in one home. This is way better in my view (for a child with two parents who are a positive influence and who are each keen to stay involved) than the alternative of a conventional separated family structure.

Challenges for wider family in acceptance

Generally-speaking, my advice when responding to the criticism, comment or even just well-meant input from those outside of your separated family is to pay it little attention if you find it contradictory to your views. There will always be those who feel it their business to offer an opinion or judgement on the choices others make. Their comments are more likely a reflection of their own biases and values rather than a considered opinion on what might be best for you and your kids in your life.

The one caveat to this advice is in managing the challenges presented for your wider family (primarily your parents and siblings who may well be close to your kids). The challenges they experience and the things they feel about your choices are likely to result in them sharing their opinion with you. I feel that generally it's important to take note of these opinions out of courtesy and love, even if you don't agree with them.

As with other aspects of divorce, the opinions of these relatives are only likely to matter to you if you love your family, value their input and want to ensure that their relationship with your kids continues uninterrupted. This has always been the case for me.

I'm very fortunate that in spite of her not getting along with my parents particularly well during the course of our marriage (or since divorcing), my ex has always been co-operative in continuing to allow and even enable the kids in visiting with my family. The same has also been true in regard to me encouraging the ongoing contact between my kids and her extended family. Moving to a nesting model of parenting hasn't had any effect on this. My family frequently come to visit with me and the kids when I'm resident parent in the nest, and I'm aware that my ex mother-in-law and sister-in-law often come and visit at the nest when my ex is in residence.

I mention the aspect of challenge in this chapter in relation to wider family, since nesting could conceivably be a source of fear or frustration for your family to observe. They may consider from their vantage point, that you and your ex forming a closer living arrangement than others may feel is sustainable or even practical for a divorced couple, which could be harmful or upsetting. They may fear further pain or upset for you or your kids arising from the setup. Of course, they're justified in feeling this way, being driven first and foremost out of love for you and your kids.

In my experience, the best means of handling this challenge is to bypass it from the outset. The true proof that will most effectively assuage the fears of your wider family is in seeing you approach and manage the nesting arrangement in a business-like and consistent fashion. If you demonstrate that this is a set-up that is geared around the needs of your kids, and putting the kids' needs to the fore, then no well-meaning family member will possibly object or have legitimate cause to fear the setup or yours or your ex's motives.

I can't emphasize enough the importance of respecting and valuing the input of your close family, assuming that you have a close relationship with them. Always remember that they love and care for you and your kids and it will likely have been painful for them to see you going through divorce and adapting to your new way of life. This is equally true even if your marriage was a miserable one and they were delighted when you announced it was ending.

The simple reality is that families can say the wrong thing sometimes, even though they're usually driven by the best and purest of motives. Nesting is a non-traditional setup and it may be that they initially struggle to understand how it could work. Be patient with them as you explain how you intend to make it work and then demonstrate that you're making considered and long-term choices for your kids and I'm sure that their concerns (if they have any) will fade away.

If you *don't* have a close relationship with your wider family, then of course this advice is irrelevant to you and you won't likely be concerned over their opinion.

Challenges for your new partner (or when you return to dating)

The final area of potential difficulty that I want to explore here is likely to be come up some time after your divorce (by rights, it shouldn't come up from the outset); it's in the challenges that nesting can present when you and/or your ex start dating other people. If you're interested to read my views on when and how to make this happen in your life, then you can pick up my book on this topic at a later stage. I'd recommend though at a minimum that you should be certain you are through all the stages of healing after your divorce before you so much as contemplate setting up an online dating profile or think about dating again! This process could easily take a year or more once your divorce is final and formalised.

When we started our nesting arrangement, both my ex and I had long-since remarried to other people so the challenge that could arise in this context was never a consideration for us. I imagine however that it might have been something to consider if either she or I had been single but also in the midst of dating. The key point worthy of emphasising, is that in my view, kids shouldn't be aware of anyone that you or your ex are dating until long after the relationship is proven and established for the long-term. By long-term, my simple guidance and that which was formulated from advice given to me and also painful experiences in my life post-divorce, means at least a year after your first meet and start dating someone new. This is how long it takes (in my opinion) to be certain of the long-term future of a relationship.

By definition then, if you follow this guidance it means that your kids are unlikely to meet anyone you are casually dating purely by virtue of the nesting arrangement until long after you're certain that person is to become a long-term fixture in your life. As difficult as it can sometimes be to allow a new relationship to flourish within the confines of a divorced relationship, particularly for a parent who has little time to themselves, it's my view that your dating activities need to be carried out when the kids aren't with you, no matter how old the kids are. If you're committed to nesting or even 50-50 co-parenting, then you will have ample time (50% of your life or thereabouts) when you are free of child-caring responsibility in which to pursue your dating life.

I may sound puritanical in this to some extent, but I say it on the basis that I've observed it is harmful for kids to keep seeing people coming and going in the lives of their parents. Such experiences seem only to teach them that relationships and people will come and go into their lives and cannot be relied upon. It also heaps on extra pain for them if they are to become attached to someone who you are dating, only later to lose that person from their lives if your relationship fails.

I believe it's essential that the nesting arrangement needs to be treated by you and by anyone you are dating as an immovable commitment in your life that blocks out much of your time. If you are contemplating introducing someone into your life and your kids' lives, then I'm assuming that you believe that there is a long-term future for the relationship. For this to happen I believe it's essential to protect your co-parenting arrangement and the nesting structure from outside influence or comment (golden rule number 14!) and as such the arrangement needs to be accepted by the new person in your life if the relationship is to stand a chance of enduring.

I believe that this is quite a black and white situation and am categorical in my advice on this. It is of course your choice over whether you take it on-board or not.

When your ex is dating

A further challenge that you may have to confront at some stage, and which could provoke difficult feelings will stem from how you feel knowing that your ex is dating and prospectively having a new partner to stay with them in the nest during their week of occupancy. The emotions prompted by this are likely to be very similar to those you would feel generally in regard to your ex moving on and dating again. An inevitable difference however is the fact that you are on some level sharing living space with them via the nest. Only you can really determine how you feel about that.

The degree to which this is a problem for you may well only become apparent as and when this becomes a factor in your nesting arrangement. How you *think* you will feel about it and how you *actually* feel about it should it ever occur are likely to be different.

There will undoubtedly be a number of intricacies that will be unique to your post-divorce life. I would hope though, that as two communicative people who are focused on the needs of their kids first and foremost, that you will have had conversations at the outset of your nesting arrangement that have covered topics such as:

- **Setting of ground rules for how soon you will each introduce your kids to future prospective partners.** Like I've said above, my guidance is to not do this for 12 months or more, to ensure you are convinced of the longevity of the relationship before the kids become involved. You may well disagree with this guidance, and that is of course your right. Either way, I'd suggest you discuss with your ex either a set-timeframe, or at least discuss with them when you have found someone significant and want them to meet your kids, *before* making the introduction. You will jointly be able to decide if you feel the kids are ready to meet someone new.

- **Agreeing principles about if and when either of you will have future partners to stay at the nest.** This is important to discuss mainly in the context of its impact on the kids. However, as you will each be sharing the space of the nest (even if not at the same time) then it would be useful to have a mutual agreement and ground rules over having other partners to stay at the nest. It is home for you both, after all!

Taken as a whole I hope you can see that the challenges that are potentially presented by nesting after divorce can each be managed and overcome if your will and desire is strong enough to do so.

With every endeavour, there will be things that are challenging, difficult and non-ideal but we have the choice to use these as justifications against taking further action. Alternatively, we can take them as opportunities to test ourselves, to grow and put in the required effort to overcome them.

Some of these challenges will be purely for you to overcome individually, whereas others are likely to be for both you and your ex to tackle after agreeing an approach. Whichever you feel apply in your post-divorce life, I hope that giving them due consideration and forethought.

Regardless of the potential challenges that may exist, you'll still feel inspired to give nesting a go if you feel there is a significant benefit to be gained for you and your kids.

Chapter Seven -
Practical Considerations and Concessions

In this chapter I wanted to spend some time discussing some of the other considerations that have had to be evaluated, weighed-up or balanced as we've set up and then lived with the nesting arrangement. They have occurred at various points for us, either as we were setting-up the arrangement, or as we've progressed through the months and eventually the years of living with it.

The things that I want to mention in this section are those that need evaluating before you decide to establish the arrangement. You need to give them thought and try and foresee how you will feel about them, either now and in the short-term or as the years pass. There would be little point in me trying to convince anyone and everyone that nesting can work for them and there *are* a lot of things to weigh-up before committing to the process.

As I've mentioned earlier, the concept of nesting for our separated family was originally proposed as a solution by my ex. I don't believe at the time she was aware that this was a recognised arrangement that even had a formal name. When she mentioned the idea to me, it was obviously something that she had taken time to consider and which she felt was likely to be viable for us. It did take me quite a bit of time and soul-searching before I felt willing to give it a go. I've noted many of the considerations below, that went through my mind before agreeing to set up the arrangement.

I've tried to present them in some sort of logical order, but no matter where you are in either considering the idea for the first time, contemplating a move to nesting from conventional co-parenting or even just tweaking your own arrangement I hope that each is worthy of a little thought.

Is it viable for us?

The most fundamental consideration is in whether the arrangement really has a chance of working for you all as a separated family in practical and realistic terms. I've assumed for the most part that this is a concept with at least some chance of working for you otherwise I can't see why you might have picked up the book (other than perhaps out of curiosity)! My basic assumption about you, the reader is that you are committed to giving your kids the best possible upbringing you can, and that you are open to doing what is necessary to make this happen. This is the case regardless of how you feel about your ex, the circumstances that led to your divorce or separation, or the lasting feelings that you have in regard to your ex. Your priority and focus is presumably firmly on doing the best for your kids.

Interlaced within this assumption is that you are considering nesting for the right reasons, all fundamentally linked to giving your kids (and you, and your ex) the best life possible post-divorce.

Some examples of the *wrong* reasons for contemplating it would include the following:

- Viewing nesting as a means of maintaining close living proximity with your ex, either as a way of spying on them, keeping tabs on their movements or in the hope of eventually winning them back.
- Being driven solely by an opportunity to save money or cut your living costs.
- Being motivated by a desire to prevent your ex from moving on or meeting someone else.
- Contemplating nesting out of a sense of apathy or because it seems like too much hassle to move out fully.
- Considering nesting as a means of concocting a way out from paying support or maintenance that might be due in relation to your ex or your kids.
- Doing it as a means of appearing the bigger person or to win social points amongst friends, family or co-workers.
- As a means of conducting a social experiment so that you can write a book on it!

I can say with certainty that if your motives for nesting aren't entirely pure, and I'll state it again for clarity, *if your chief aim isn't driven by giving the kids the best childhood you can, whilst respecting and accepting that your relationship with their other parent is over,* then I can assure you that it will eventually fail.

With those purposes and intentions now clearly stated, there are a few pre-requisites that I believe would be useful to consider and evaluate before entering into the nesting arrangement.

For the kids

Age – I genuinely believe that nesting would work effectively for kids of all ages. At a *very* young age, there may be a case for the kids to be with their mother for the majority of the time assuming this is viable and necessary, for example if they were breast-feeding. Aside from such factors though, I believe that kids of all ages are equally adaptable and also perceptive about the circumstances of their lives.

It makes perfect sense to move forward and establish the new way of life after divorce for them and for you, as soon as is practical. You can do this sensitively and gradually of course, but the key is to not delay or kid yourself that you're waiting for the children to be older, more flexible, more understanding, more mature or whatever other reason you'd like to concoct. Just like the act of having kids itself, there is no perfect time. Our kids were 12 and 16 when we first started nesting and obviously quite mature. However, they were 3 and 7 when we first started equal co-parenting and I know that the arrangement has been successful and effective mainly due to it having been sustainable and consistent for most of their lives.

Siblings – Nesting would, in my opinion work as well no matter how many kids we have; it just so happens that we have two. I believe that while they fight and argue as all siblings do, they have a closer bond than many siblings have with each other. They've come and gone between their Mum and I for most of their lives, but they've been together, and a consistent feature, there for each other for *all* of their lives. That said, if you have only one child, and they have never known life with a sibling, then of course it makes little difference in either marriage or after divorce. The same goes for more than two kids in a divorced family as well.

Gender – I had a real fear as a Dad, that when my daughters' hormones took control and puberty kicked in, that my life as an effective single-parent would become untenable. I'm relieved to report that it was an unfounded fear. Whether this was due to my antiquated preconceptions which were unfounded, or simply because we've all just got on with it (enabled by a fair amount of understanding on the part of my daughters) we've made it work.

There have been the emergency missions to buy sanitary towels, the awkward conversations, the tears and the screaming (mostly theirs, occasionally mine) that have punctuated the teenage years, but we've got through it. I've also witnessed my second wife raising her eldest child, the only boy in our blended family, virtually single-handed before we met and married. She has very effectively filled the roles typically filled by a father for most of the time.

Co-parenting and nesting both demand that Mum and Dad each fill all the roles of both parents in just the same way as this is demanded in conventional divorced families. Nesting neither heightens nor reduces these demands.

For the divorced or separated parents

There is really only one consideration to make in regard to nesting, but it is rather a big one. Put simply, do you and your ex believe you can get along well enough to make it work?

Putting aside all the improper reasons why some may misguidedly consider nesting (outlined above), the key question here is as follows: Can you exist on positive (or even neutral) terms with your ex for the long-term and commit to making nesting work for your kids? Can your ex make the same commitment towards you? It doesn't demand that you are best friends. It doesn't even have to place a burden on you both to ever see each other or be in the same place at the same time if you really can't bear that idea. As mentioned previously, my ex and I often go weeks or even months without seeing each other in person or in passing, not by design but because our nesting arrangement is set up so that we never really have cause to cross paths.

The key thing though is that even at times when we've had differences to resolve, we've had the ability to put these to one side and to disentangle those from the business of raising our kids effectively. It's not always been easy, and there have been challenging times (and undoubtedly will be further differences in future). We've always managed to make it work though.

Nesting demands that you're sure that you can deal responsibly and in an adult fashion with each other for the benefit of the kids if nothing else.

Consider our nesting arrangement for a moment. There are many reasons why we need to be able to get-along and act in an appropriate manner towards each other, including:

- Trusting that each other will pay their way and not leave the other responsible for bills or rent when it's due.
- Respecting each other's privacy and not using the proximity to snoop or invade their space/lives.
- Tidying up our own mess and not leaving it for each other.
- Not using each other as a go-between to the kids and not bad-mouthing/speaking-ill of each other around the kids.
- Not eating each other's food or using their possessions without permission.
- Trusting that they'll respect our property and respecting theirs in return.
- Sharing responsibility, information and making co-operative decisions in regard to the kids.

The list could go-on with many other things, some trivial and others more significant. The point is that there is a real need to know, before you contemplate nesting that you can adopt the appropriate mind-set and attitude towards your ex in relation to these and any other requirements that might reasonably crop up now or in future. This intent is *absolutely essential* to make it work.

It can be achieved via a form of truce if you can't conclude your differences fully. You don't have to patch up all the issues you have with each other; after all you did presumably dislike each other enough to decide to part? It's unrealistic to think it'll be easy to put all differences aside. Nonetheless, you need to be resolved that as far as nesting goes, you're willing to act responsibly and respectfully in order to make it work.

This was already pre-qualified for us, by the time my ex and I considered nesting. After 10+ years of equal co-parenting we'd proven that most of these challenges were manageable for each of us. The sharing of living quarters (albeit at separate times) was the final element to be considered, but having established that we were both devoted to the kids first and foremost, the rest became easier to manage.

The purpose of nesting

I've read articles that suggest nesting would be a good way of easing the transition out of a marriage or relationship, presumably to make the process of divorce and parting easier on the kids. I'd contend that in this example that's probably only relevant for younger kids (toddlers and pre-schoolers) who might not be able to understand fully what a divorce means for them and their parents. For kids who are older, I suspect that nesting as a transitory arrangement only, would be potentially more confusing for them, and would likely simply delay and prolong the pain for the kids in adapting to their parents parting. For this reason, I suspect that as a transitory arrangement alone, nesting is probably not the best idea (in my view).

If your kids are old enough to genuinely understand the fact that you are parting, and you are each consistently communicative with them so that they understand what is happening, and why, then nesting should work well for kids of all ages.

You will of course know your kids best and understand if this applies to them. If your eventual intention is to split fully, and if long-term nesting isn't your intention for the future then it may be that this isn't the right thing for you. In my experience, when a change of any sort is planned in relation to the lives of my kids, the best approach is to get right to it, to 'rip off the sticking plaster' in one swift move and to execute the change as quickly and efficiently as possible. It should of course be planned properly and executed sensitively. The key thing is to act, and to do it quickly and consistently, with long-term goals in mind.

The ideal purpose of nesting in my view is to establish a long-term, sustainable arrangement (ideally for the entire childhood if possible) so that the kids can get used-to it, rely upon it and adapt to it as their norm, and the parents can too.

What place to use for the nest

Assuming you've established that you, your ex and the kids are likely to be able to work within the nesting arrangement, the next consideration is in choosing the home that will become the nest itself. You will need somewhere to call home (full-time for the kids, but also part-time for you and your ex). While this doesn't have to be one place for the remaining duration of their childhood, it's reasonable to not want to move too often; nobody likes moving house, do they?

We've discussed this in depth already, but in terms of location, the main pre-requisite for the location of the nest is that it enables your kids to attend the school of your choosing. In most cases this will likely be the school system they were in before your divorce; continuity in things that can be maintained during and after divorce is obviously desirable.

As I've described about my own situation, my ex and I are both remarried and our new family homes are approximately one hour's drive in opposite directions away from the town where my kids have lived their entire lives. We've chosen to maintain this as their base to the end of compulsory schooling, in spite of the fact that neither of us has any other lasting ties to the area. It's something of a paradox to me particularly that I should have ended up based in this town given that none of us (the kids included I suspect) has any long-term desire to remain there either, but that's just one of the mysteries of life I guess!

We're told that location is key to most housing decisions, and the same is true for other aspects of the nest too. Our kids have benefitted (as they've got older) from being near to public transport links too. They're able to get to and from school on their own now that they're old enough, which makes transitioning into and out of the nest a little easier for their Mum and I as the kids grow in independence. They're also close to their friends, lifelong family friends and also familiar with the area, all of which have helped to make the arrangement less scary and more sustainable for them.

As for the parents, it really matters very little where you are when you're not the custodial parent, living in at the nest. I would guess that most won't want to frequently travel ridiculous distances, when they're not living with the kids, but my ex and I both have jobs where we travel a lot, nationally and sometimes (in my case) internationally. I've built my career while managing to maintain the commitment that I'd always be there for the girls when they were on 'my week'. This hasn't been a constraint to my career or my life and I would encourage you to maintain your career aspirations too. Where your will is strong, you'll likely find a way to make it happen.

Benefits and drawbacks of using the former family home

I've read of examples where divorcing families made the former family home into the nest; the kids got custody of the house! This has also been covered in depth earlier.

I can see some benefits in this scenario. There is potentially less of a shock of adapting to new surroundings, or of having to go through the forced-trauma of moving house on top of changes in family structure. There would also presumably be a comfort factor and a small trade-off for the kids in maintaining the same space. On the other side of this, I can imagine that it would also be somewhat confusing a distinction to make for the kids, depending on their ages, to adapt to the idea that they are still living in the family home. Mum and Dad are still both occasionally living there with them, and yet the parents are no longer together? This could conceivably be a bit more difficult to understand for the kids. It may also prolong the process for the parents of adapting to being parted, too.

I can imagine if I'd had to keep coming and going to the former family home for alternate weeks after our divorce, it could have been psychologically and emotionally challenging and potentially have prolonged the pain for me, as well as for the kids, I suspect.

I would also assume that there could be excessive financial costs associated with maintaining a former family home when it's now going to be used by one less adult on a weekly basis. The family home may not have been that extravagant to begin with, but it would still likely be larger than is required for a nest, and hence add a further burden of cost on the nesting arrangement.

I'm not categorically against the use of the former family home as the nest but I maintain that it's certainly not necessary to think that it must be retained to make the arrangement work. There may also be better and more appropriate properties available that are better suited to nesting and I've already talked about the characteristics of our apartment that I feel make it ideal in comparison to the more conventional family home we had when married.

Space requirements – Benefits and drawbacks of each parent having their own space

I'm fortunate to feel that we have what seems to be the ideal property for nesting purposes, and will remain there for the duration of the arrangement (until child number 2 finishes her compulsory education and goes to University, or moves out to make her way in the world). We didn't start out in this property though, and the first place we used hadn't been secured for the purpose of nesting.

Put simply, the first place was just too small.

It's not that the nest needs to be super-spacious, but there is definitely a slightly greater space requirement that is brought about by both parents quite reasonably wanting to leave a few possessions at the nest when they're not there. For example, we both provide food for the weeks when we're custodial parent; I've no desire to bring every crumb of food with me each week, so I leave a stock of items there in cupboards that are mine alone. She has her own cupboards and does the same. I like to leave some clothes there too; a business suit for work (in case a meeting comes up at short notice), some gym gear and running shoes, a sweatshirt and coat, and so-on. We also both use the same bed but with our own bedding, pillows, blankets and so-on. I strip the bedding when I leave on a Monday morning and she does the same the following week. I don't want to have to pack my car with pillows, blankets and the other bedding when I leave, nor bring it with me when I come back the following week, so it lives in the bottom of my wardrobe space and she does the same with hers.

For the storage of all these things, and the inevitable books, DVDs, electrical devices, chargers and so-on that each of us wants to leave there, it's necessary to have just a bit of wardrobe space, or a few drawers that can be used for storage on a long term basis.

What also became apparent when we first moved to nesting, was that the girls had quite a few duplicate possessions due to our preference for them not to cart loads of stuff between homes when we were equal co-parenting from separate homes. For a time, while rationalisation happened, it was also natural to expect that we needed space to accommodate all the essentials.

When a suitable property came up, we recognised that it had all the things that our first nest was missing and so we pounced upon it.

We now have a reasonably large communal living space, with a corner equipped as a home-office for the parent of the week, with desk, desk-chair, laptop stand and monitor; we both work from home from time-to-time. The kids both have their own bedrooms, and the third bedroom is for the parent-of-the-week. We're lucky that the apartment has a bathroom for each bedroom and so each of the kids, and the parent-of-the-week has their own bathroom. Ours is en-suite and this makes the parents quarters self-contained. It's not essential, but with two teenage girls, both fond of preening and pampering for hours on end, the bathroom situation is a blessing for me!

Separate bedrooms for the parents

One final consideration about the space is in whether it might be preferable for the parents to each have their own bedroom to use when they are at the nest. You'll recall that when my ex floated the idea originally, she had thought that her rental property with 4 bedrooms would be ideal in that she and I could have each had a space. This never came to fruition but in retrospect it prompted me to consider whether it would have been advantageous to have my own room in the nest, separate to hers.

The conclusion I reached was that it wouldn't have been, and I want to share the reasoning behind that.

Many might feel awkward about notionally 'sharing' a bed with their ex. I say sharing but only to the degree that she sleeps on it one week, I use it the next. To my mind, it's no different than sleeping in a hotel bed where some complete stranger has slept in it the night before. Like a hotel we change the bedding for our use, and as such it's no different in my mind and not advantageous to any significant degree to have a bed that's mine and mine-alone.

Furthermore, even if I had my own room and she had hers, I don't believe that I would leave more of my stuff there, or feel any more, or less at home in it than I do in using the parent-of-the-week's room. That's my space when I'm there, and hers when she's there. It's never *our* room. It's a subtle, but important distinction to make.

The final factor for me is that when the nest is mine for the week, at the weekends my second wife and the step-kids will come and stay and we have the whole blended family living there. Sometimes when it's mine to use, and the kids aren't there for example if they're away on vacation with their Mum, then me and my wife will use it to entertain friends and family who may stay there with us. We use all the space as though it's ours and ours alone when we're in residence. I would feel decidedly *less comfortable* using the home as our own if one room was permanently off-limits due to it being my ex's room, left as though she'd just popped out for groceries!

It's a subtle distinction and it isn't a reflection on me needing the nest to have been swept of all trace of my ex in order to be able to relax there. It's merely another way in which it helps to keep the focus on it being the kids home first and foremost. My ex and I slot in around the kids, but it's also our own home when we're there too, and it's important that it feels as such. This is one way in which we make that happen.

In conclusion then I don't believe a separate bedroom for each of the parents is necessary to make nesting work.

Frequency/interval of parent swapping

Many of the logistical considerations around nesting are common to the considerations around co-parenting generally. The model that we've practiced has been equal co-parenting 50-50, one week on, one week off but this is not always feasible, or even desirable for other families.

50-50 may not be feasible

There may be many circumstances where for a variety of good reasons one or other parent isn't able to commit to 50% and this is fine. Some careers demand that one parent may be unable to flex their work to enable part-time single parenting, and without their income the financial stability of the separated family is untenable. An example of this would be if one parent was an airline parent (to pick just one career). Their work demands of them that they could be away for a period of days at a time, and this is just a fact of life. It doesn't mean that their kids can't benefit from co-parenting and while the switch of responsibility could mean that 7-days on, 7-days off as parent isn't feasible, it's still possible for the parents to alternate responsibility of parenting on a regular basis.

I've encountered other families practising nesting where reasons have determined that a more conventional involvement is appropriate. One or other parent has lived with the kids in the nest Monday to Friday, and the other parent moves into the nest as custodial parent for the weekends. During this time, the first parent ex goes somewhere else for the weekend. This has generally also been driven by the demands of work and would typically fit for a family where one parent had a job that demanded they be elsewhere for work, Monday to Friday. Their input to the raising of their kids, while maybe not strictly even in terms of hours put in with the kids, is presumably still beneficial for the kids, particularly when it's part of the overall picture of co-operative co-parenting and nesting.

Fundamentally there is no rule to say that co-parenting has to be split on a 50-50 basis between both parents. It's just the simplest way (in my view) of conceptually ensuring that each parent does their bit, but also receives equal opportunity to spend time with the kids. What is more important than the actual numbers, is that both parents feel that the agreed split of responsibility, and corresponding agreement of financial and logistical support that each receives is fair and equitable all round.

An underlying fairness and equity will ensure that the arrangement is sustainable and lasting which is, after all, the most important thing to strive for. If it's not equitable, then there's a good chance that resentments and anger will bubble beneath the surface and eventually spill-over. This could then threaten the future of the arrangement and undermine it, which is obviously best avoided.

Structure and consistency

I've talked above about some of the means of dividing up parental responsibility where a 50-50 split is not viable for whatever reason. It's not an absolute pre-requisite, however I do feel strongly that part of what makes co-parenting and bird-nesting into a sustainable and long-term solution for parenting after divorce is for the arrangement to be designed in such a way as to be structured and consistent. This is emphasized in a number of my aforementioned golden rules of shared and co-parenting, most notably rules two and five.

Structure is important, and I think that most people, even those who like to think of themselves as easy-going and flexible appreciate a bit of structure in their lives. This is particularly true for kids. To appreciate why, consider what's at stake for the kids who are likely to have weathered your divorce. They've witnessed the split of their parents who they'd subconsciously relied upon being features in their lives forever. You can understand why the structure and reliability of other aspects of their lives becomes even more important after divorce.

Structure in your nesting arrangement means that there is an understood pattern for the kids first and foremost, regarding which parent is going to be in the home with them when they wake up in the morning. It's about them knowing that the absent parent who they are presumably yearning to see, will be with them again in a few days. It's about giving them comfort in knowing who will be looking after them, and when.

For the parents, structure also offers enormous benefit in enabling them to plan their lives and manage their careers and other commitments accordingly. Working shift patterns and business travel can, and should be planned around when you are committed to being there for the kids, if such activities are not possible when you're based at the nest. Social commitments can be managed and planned around the times when you have the kids (either to include them or not as appropriate). Structure and predictability make it easier to plan and predict where you will be, what you will be doing and when.

The consistency of the arrangement ties closely to structure. Not only is structure and repeatability of value, but consistency of the arrangement is significant too, if it's going to be a sustainable solution for parenting.

Both parents need to be committed to making it work for the long-term, and consistently show-up to the arrangement when they need to. This isn't just about logistically turning up and being there on the designated date and time. It's about treating your parenting commitments as immovable and as something that generally won't be changed.

When you're committed to the arrangement, you must do it whole-heartedly and for the long-haul. It's a commitment to your kids and to being there as they need, expect and deserve you to be.

I'm assuming that your commitment to the arrangement isn't at question given that you're progressive enough to be thinking about co-parenting and nesting for your divorced family. I've mentioned this here since it's a long-term commitment, not something that you can allow yourself to become less enthusiastic about. It's not easy, but then nothing worthwhile ever is.

Financials

A big consideration amongst many aspects and facets of divorce is in relation to the financial side of the process. I've discussed separately in this book how nesting can be either a means of reducing costs of living (as was the case for us) or of increasing these depending on what your circumstances are and the choices you make in the process. In real terms, like anything in life you have the flexibility and choice to make things work based on sacrifices you might need to make. Costs of nesting can't be completely pared back, but you can certainly make choices about how you get the arrangement in place and make it work. If you're committed to making it work, you'll be able to find a way to balance the books. Put simply, we *all* have the ability to cut costs or make more money if we're sufficiently committed to do so.

There are a few other financial considerations to be made as you contemplate and then set up your nesting arrangement.

Are you able to separate the financial terms of your wider divorce from the finances associated with your nesting? - In common with my guidance in other books I've written regarding co-parenting, I feel it's extremely helpful to consider the funding of your co-parenting and nesting as entirely separate from the wider terms of your divorce. You may have agreed a financial settlement from one party to the other to redistribute assets, debt or income. While this may be something that was done willingly, or something that one or both of you feel embittered about, it's helpful to draw a line under this as far as agreeing the terms of your nesting agreement between you.

Nesting requires you to each contribute to the funding of the nest, ideally by funding it equally or at least in proportion to the amount of input and income you each bring to the arrangement. However you may agree the split of costs (which will include a share of the rent, utility bills, local taxes and so-on), you both need to feel that it's fair and equitable. If not, resentments will creep in and undermine the arrangement and your confidence in it.

Do you trust your ex from a financial perspective? - This isn't a suggestion to treat your ex with contempt or to question their scruples, but you need to feel assured that they'll act fairly and responsibly within the arrangement (and you must be committed to doing so too). If you agree that you're going to split the electricity bill equally (for example) but you are constantly suspicious that your ex will be running the heating and leaving the windows open when you're not there, and are fearful that your share of the cost will hurt you financially, then this too will undermine your faith in the agreement. Trust them, and expect them to trust you back.

If you have a history of not being able to trust your ex from a financial perspective, either because they reneged on their financial commitments in the past, or because they have a questionable history of poor financial commitment then this too is something that at least warrants some consideration and discussion. Your financial future is going to be tied to their conduct to some degree as long as you are using nesting to raise your kids. It's better that you air and discuss concerns from the off, rather than letting potential resentments or issues simmer behind the scenes.

How does your new partner feel about it?

This issue for consideration will largely depend on where you are in the process of divorce and nesting. I'd suggest that whether you are considering nesting and are just at the outset of life after divorce, or whether you are considering it after a number of years apart from your ex, then in either case you are to be commended for putting the needs of your kids to the fore. However, it's an obvious fact that you're likely to only be contemplating the feelings of a new partner if you've been divorced for some time and have eventually moved on to find someone else to spend your life with.

It's natural that people move on after divorce. Even if you've newly parted and are convinced that you are sworn-off relationships for life, or destined to remain alone forever, you may well find that things change as the months and years pass. I felt pretty resistant to new relationships at the infancy of my post-divorce life, and yet here I sit now, married to my second wife for over three years and counting. Life moves on, people move on, you will too. If you're interested in my thoughts and guidance on dating and relationships after divorce, then you'll find my book on the subject where you got hold of this one.

I'll assume that if this consideration applies to you because you've been parted for at least a while and are considering the feelings of someone who is significant to you and who you believe you will be with for the long term. At the risk of stating the obvious, I wanted to make this assumption clear as the first and most important people in this consideration are your kids. You are their parent for life, and naturally what should matter most is their needs and what they require from you. They were here first and, bluntly, their needs come first in my view.

Assuming you're in a long-term relationship with someone following your divorce, it's important in many respects, not just in relation to nesting that the role of your kids in your life is maintained on a pedestal as untouchable and not-to-be-influenced by your new partner. This sentiment is represented in Golden rule number 13 of shared and co-parenting. It is essential that you protect your parenting arrangement from outside influence or corruption. If they are the right person, and decent and moral then I see no reason why anyone would want to stand in the way of any divorced parent looking to do their best by raising their kids.

Unfortunately, I know from first-hand experience that this is not always the case and factors such as jealousy and obstruction from your new partner are going to prevent co-parenting or nesting from being a possibility. This was a lesson learned during another relationship between my marriages. If you fear this is the case for you, then maybe you need to reconsider your new relationship, or reconsider co-parenting or nesting. I hope you put your kids first.

This consideration is not all doom and gloom though. The example of my own co-parenting and subsequent nesting is an example of how it can be made to work with the input and acceptance of a supportive new partner.

When I met my second wife (via an online dating website as it happens), I stated up front that my kids demanded a large portion of my time, attention and resources. I was also at pains to share that I have a closer relationship with my ex-wife than many divorcees do, by virtue of the fact that we've decided to co-operatively raise the kids of our relationship. This contrasted with my new wife's life in relation to her ex and the fact that she has custody of her kids for most of the time and they visit for occasional weekends with their Dad. In spite of this, she has always been accepting of the arrangement and taken time to build a bond with my kids as I have with hers.

When we met, I was co-parenting my kids and they would live in my house half the time and with their Mum for the other half. This meant that my new wife got used to mainly seeing me on alternate weeks. For the first year of our relationship in fact it was *only* when I didn't have my kids that we spent time together; we wanted to take a year to see if our relationship was going to last before meeting each other's kids.

Rolling time forwards a few years, when we eventually decided to move in together it was a question of whether to amalgamate our blended family in a single location, moving her kids out of school to live with me and mine (who are older than hers), or whether we preserved our main family home where she was. In this scenario I would remain with mine on alternate weeks to see out the duration of my co-parenting commitment until my kids reached adulthood. For a variety of reasons, we chose the latter option, mainly I suppose because we have no longer-term aspiration to base ourselves in the town where my kids have grown up. The move of her kids to a different school system for the second time since her divorce also seemed an unnecessary additional change for them to adapt to.

Subsequent to this decision, the prospect of nesting was first floated by my ex, and my new wife was the first to get on board with the idea. She's certainly not the jealous type which helps enormously. She's also pragmatic and could see the numerous benefits that existed for my kids and also financially for us in the arrangement as was being discussed.

We've gone on to adapt to the situation and have lived with it since. I still stay at the nest for alternate weeks, away from my second wife and step-kids. The full blended family (all 6 of us) will often get together at weekends in those weeks, sometimes at the family home, sometimes at the nest. We all flex, compromise and make it work and accept that this is an intricacy of our unusual family set up. In the weeks when I'm not parenting at the nest, I live in the family home with my wife and step-kids. This arrangement and pattern will remain until my daughters have both left home to go to university. At that point, who knows where life will take us but the default would be that I move in with the wife and step-kids full time for a few more years until they are adults. After that, the world is my oyster to explore with my wife!

This rather convoluted explanation of my situation hopefully illustrates to you that regardless of your circumstances and the complexities within it, nesting can be made to work in a variety of scenarios. This all depends on the strength of your desire to be flexible and make it work. Certainly, there are some scenarios that I don't believe are pragmatic or compatible with nesting, but it's a viable alternative for many.

How do your family feel?

In this context I am referring to your wider family, your parents, siblings, grandparents or any other relatives (or close friends) and how they may prospectively feel about your co-parenting and nesting. We've already discussed this from the perspective of the challenges it can bring for them, and for you as you make nesting a feature of your post-divorce life.

The well-meant feelings and input from those we love and who love us, can be a valuable source of insight, support and input to difficult decisions and in good times and bad. I'd hope you've benefited from this during the course of your divorce and at other times when you've needed it. We must also be careful at times when taking into consideration such support and opinion since at times there is at least a small risk that this can be clouded by the opinions and prejudices of those who provide it. This is particularly the case when you've divorced from the person who they may now resent or dislike to some degree.

Even if you've been able to patch over your differences with your ex to the extent that you're now contemplating nesting, it may well be that the lasting feelings of anger, resentment or hurt still exist for your close family and friends. If those people were there for you, helping you through times of difficulty and pain, they've likely seen at first-hand or heard from you of all the wrongs committed by your ex, when you were at your most upset. It is naturally hard then for them to contemplate a non-traditional arrangement such as co-parenting or nesting which will likely preserve far more input from your ex in the lives of you and your kids than your wider family may feel is helpful or healthy.

I would never advocate ignoring the advice of those who offer it with the right intentions, particularly not family and friends who want for you and your kids to be happy in life. However, it is essential that if you have the courage of your convictions regarding your decision to use co-parenting or nesting, that you take on-board their input and opinion but treat it as just that. Don't treat it as a judgment of others whose opinion should overrule yours. It is yours and your kids' lives that are important here, and which will be affected by the nesting process. If you believe it's the right thing and will serve the intended purpose for you all then that is what matters. Treat the advice of others and those who offer it with kindness and respect but don't be swayed if you feel that they just don't seem to *get it*.

To share my own experience, I'm lucky that my family have always been extremely supportive towards me in life, and particularly so in the years following my divorce. When I initially divorced, I'm sure they were equally concerned for my welfare and also for the kids, as well as fearful for their future access to the kids. As it has happened, to the credit of my ex while she and my family have had their differences, she has always appreciated the role of my wider family in the lives of the girls and never stood in the way of their access.

When our co-parenting arrangement was put in place, they supported me in getting it going, and in visiting to help with the kids at regular intervals, as well as helping during school holidays. As we've moved to the nesting arrangement, I'm pleased to report that this has also continued with my parents coming to visit and stay at the nest for the occasional weekend. I realise that this all sounds quite mundane in the context of family relationships after divorce. It is nothing out of the ordinary and this is the main point really; a nesting arrangement seems to me, on most fronts to allow for a completely conventional post-divorce family life to go on uninterrupted. It's an unusual arrangement but life goes on completely as normal once it's embedded.

When it might not be feasible

Whilst you may believe that I have an agenda to promote in writing this book, I am by no means trying to push bird-nesting as the one and only way of effectively raising kids in a separated family. I know that one-size most definitely does not fit all, and there are far too many variables at play including the personalities involved. The circumstances and causes of divorce and numerous other factors also mean that each separated family's needs will be subtly different from the next.

My aim with the book is to describe how bird-nesting works, not conceptually, but first hand, based on my own experience not just as an experiment but as part of the process that I've used to raise my own kids. It's not a scientific or theoretical social exercise, but the culmination of the experiences of my life.

I've a strong personal opinion that too many divorcees and in particular, divorced parents effectively resign themselves to a sub-standard life, or a life of just getting-by. This also applies in relation to their lives as parents after divorce. I believe that if people are aware of other, better ways of tackling particular situations (such as how to give kids a supportive, fulfilling, loving and happy childhood after divorce) through examples such as mine, then their eyes may be opened to new possibilities and their aspirations correspondingly raised.

With all that said, my aim in this book is to allow you to decide if nesting will or *won't* work for you in your separated family. I've tried to be objective throughout the book and present honest, unbiased examples and scenarios as well as sharing my own experiences.

When it comes to considering the circumstances when it might *not* be feasible, I am really, genuinely struggling to think of many examples. It doesn't mean it will work universally for everyone, but to my mind that's a good reason for everyone to at least consider it!

Blended family

Assuming both parents are legally and morally able to have a permanent relationship with the kids, the only scenario I can see that would make nesting difficult, when translated to my own life would be in the following scenario.

You'll recall my description of how my second marriage came to be, and the living arrangement that we now have. When my second wife and I met, if we'd decided that she should move into the home that I'd been using to co-parent my girls for alternate weeks, then that may have complicated things. While that would have demanded that she move her kids to the same school as mine, we could feasibly have established a new family home together. My daughters would have simply come and gone for their weeks with me as usual. In such a scenario, this then means that it would have been impossible to transition to nesting, since there's no way that me, my wife and step-kids could move in and out every other week to allow my ex to live there!

The situation would have been the same had my second-wife and I gone on to have a child together. In either scenario it would have added complexity and inflexibility to an already complex situation, which would have largely prevented nesting.

On this basis, I'd suggest that the below three scenarios are those best suited to a nesting arrangement:

1) Where the divorced parents are each single and happy to move in and out of the nest for alternative weeks, and able to live elsewhere when not residing in the nest

2) Where the divorced parents are in new relationships and happy to move in and out of the nest for alternative weeks alone or with their new partner *(assuming the other partner doesn't have kids of their own)*. They are also able to live elsewhere when not residing in the nest.

3) Where the divorced parents are in new relationships and happy to move in and out of the nest for alternate weeks *alone* while their new partner and any other kids within the blended family remain elsewhere in another home. This is the scenario describing my situation.

Hopefully you'd agree that this represents a significant range of scenarios that may be suited to nesting when considered in this context. That, really is the point. There are many considerations to be made, and most divorces will be different. However, there really exist a great number of opportunities to employ some or all of the principles of nesting and/or co-parenting and to see the corresponding benefits emerge in your lives.

Chapter Eight - What Happens Next?

By now, you've hopefully figured out whether nesting can work for you and your kids, or whether it's not the right option for you. If the latter is the case, then I'd hope that with an awareness of what's possible, an appreciation of the positive effects it can have and an understanding of the challenges that need to be overcome, that you may return to nesting as an option in future.

Even if there's no possible way that it could ever work for you, I'm deeply grateful to you for taking the time to learn about it. Too many people go through divorce and buy-in to a mind-set of acceptance and grim-determination to survive and get-by in life. They believe that this is all they can hope to achieve, and all that they can hope to expect. This is NOT the case. What's really corrosive about this is that the ethos then permeates into their kids and starts to shape the kids' expectations of life as well.

Nesting doesn't have to be the way you raise your kids after divorce to give them happy and loving childhoods. You don't have to co-parent them to raise happy, functioning and fulfilled young adults. Even if you are able to remember golden rule number 1, and routinely put the needs of your kids to the fore in all decisions that could affect them, then that is a supremely positive step that will deliver enormous benefit for you all.

Life is a constant process of change, chaos and evolution. All divorcees have a choice about how to live after divorce, both as individuals and as parents. What was once conventional and the norm doesn't have to remain so forever. Co-parenting and nesting are two ways that parents can still give their kids a happy childhood; just because the marriage failed, it doesn't have to mean the parent-child relationships degrade too. There are positive outcomes that can arise from taking new and innovative approaches to life.

If you decide to give bird-nesting a go, then I applaud you. If it's not for you, then I still applaud you for exploring alternative ways to better yours and your kids' lives. Whatever choices you make for the future, I wish you well, and hope that yours is a life of fulfilment and happiness.

Yours in gratitude,

Toby Hazlewood

Appendix -
Our House Rules:

1. We do not have a maid, butler or housekeeper – we all need to pitch-in and clean up after ourselves

2. Shoes aren't to be worn around the apartment. The carpets have been cleaned and we want to keep them clean as long as possible.

3. Clean up after yourself
   a. Don't leave cups or mugs in your room, or dishes by the sink – Wash them yourself.
   b. Don't leave dirty clothes on your floor – either they're clean enough to be worn again and can be put away until then, or they are dirty and require washing in which case put them in the laundry basket
   c. Put away clean clothes in your drawers or wardrobe
   d. See Rule number 1 if in any doubt how to handle a decision

4. If you use something, put it away or switch it off when you're done with it
   a. Food packets get put in the cupboard or the bin if empty
   b. If you mean to throw something away, put it IN the bin, not on it or near it.
   c. The TV, lamps and lights get turned off
   d. See Rule number 1

5. Please put your things back in your room rather than leaving them laying around (hair bands and pins, books, school bags etc). We have communal space and individual space and don't need to have everything all spread around the whole space

6. When clean washing is put in your room, please do the decent thing and put it away in your drawers or in your wardrobe. It is literally the least you can do.

7. Your room is your room but please show respect for the home by keeping it tidy.
   a. Make your bed and put things away
   b. Don't leave piles or rubbish or hair everywhere
   c. Don't leave cups, glasses or plates in your room. Return them to the kitchen and wash them.
   d. See Rule number 1

8. Once per week, please assist in cleaning the apartment
   a. Dust your room

b. Hoover your room

c. Clean your bathroom

Thanks and enjoy your stay!

The Management (Dad and Mum)

About the Author

Toby Hazlewood is a father, husband, author, coach and cycling enthusiast living in the North West of England. Toby is also founder of Divorced Lifestyle Design, a collective with the following mission:

"To serve with diligence and empathy those who are facing times of challenge, uncertainty and volatility as they embark on divorce or separation, by sharing inspiration, information, instruction and tactics formulated by those who have successfully navigated these challenges and gone on to thrive and not just survive."

Having parted from his first wife in 2006, Toby has co-parented the two daughters from that relationship for over 10 years and is a passionate believer in the effectiveness of co-parenting. Toby advocates a post-divorce lifestyle that allows divorcees to aspire to, establish and maintain a happy and fulfilled life, the best life possible as the best version of themselves.

His purpose is to share the tools, tactics and mind-set that will propel those currently going through divorce or separation along the journey to thriving in life rather than settling for surviving, getting-by or merely recovering.

You can learn more and access further products and services via:

toby@divorcedlifestyledesign.com - Email

Divorcedlifestyledesign.com - Blog

Facebook.com/divorcedlifestyledesigner – Facebook Community

Other books by Toby Hazlewood

If you enjoyed this book I'd love to hear from you by email to understand how it helped you and would welcome you leaving a review for it on Amazon. Even if you didn't enjoy it or find it helpful I'd still welcome your feedback; I'm here to help!

I've written a few other books that may also be useful or of interest. Feel free to pick them up on Amazon.

Shared Parenting: Successfully sharing custody of children 50-50 in separated relationships – This book tells the story of my divorce and shares the details of how me and my ex-wife decided upon and ultimately set-up a 50-50 co-parenting arrangement for our two daughters. The book identifies my golden rules for sharing parenting after divorce and describes the lessons that have been learned in over 10 years of living with the arrangement.

Shared Parenting Workbook: Sharing-parenting after Divorce – What is it, how does it work and will it work for you? – This is a condensed workbook that outlines the golden rules of shared and co-parenting after divorce and helps the reader to consider whether it may be feasible as a parenting structure in their separated family. Whilst 50-50 co-parenting may not be feasible for all, the core-principles are certainly valid and valuable for all separated families in giving the kids the best childhood possible, not one that is somehow second best.

90-Day Playbook for Thriving After Divorce – With one of the biggest uncertainties for those going through divorce being acknowledged as the role of time; to get through the pain, to feel better and to build a new life, this book provides a focussed and targeted guide to navigating divorce in 90-day chunks. The book is punchy, practically focused and applicable and is intended to guide the reader in setting the foundations for their new and ideal life in the most effective and efficient way possible.

Successful Dating and Relationships After Divorce – Even those who are resolutely single or determined (or resigned) to a life alone following divorce, may eventually find themselves considering a new relationship or at least a return to dating. This book distils my own experiences of dating and relationships after divorce. It helps the reader to recognise when they're ready to date again, how to approach dating (especially if they have kids) and how to navigate the sometimes challenging world of online dating.

Made in the USA
San Bernardino, CA
23 January 2019